MY TIME IN SPACE

My Time in Space

TIM ROBINSON

THE LILLIPUT PRESS
DUBLIN

First published 2001 by
THE LILLIPUT PRESS LTD
62–63 Sitric Road, Arbour Hill,
Dublin 7, Ireland
www.lilliputpress.ie

A CIP record for this title is available from
The British Library.

1 3 5 7 9 10 8 6 4 2

ISBN 1 901866 64 5

*The Lilliput Press receives financial assistance
from An Chomhairle Ealaíon / The Arts Council of Ireland.*

Set in Bembo
Printed by ColourBooks, Baldoyle, Dublin

CONTENTS

MY TIME IN SPACE

BIRDLIFE
(AND A PREFACE)

It's the wise thrush that knows its own song …

While my mother-to-be was lying in wait for me, a thrush sang unceasingly outside her hospital window, day after day. She told me this when I was grown up and her mind was rambling back through the past, and I have interiorized it as a seminal event, the second, to be precise, of my life. Such parental tales of one's own beginnings, which one can no longer distinguish from memories, acquire the tremendum of legend, of revealed religion. The totem animal's song enters the bloodstream via the umbilical cord; later the blood will answer to a call from outside. When I was about eleven, as near as I can guess, my mother told me that since I could fly I should go and live with the birds. I remember standing at the back door, full of the pathos of leaving home, looking at sparrows in a hawthorn tree.

That was a dream, but the idea that I could fly had seeped into my waking life. I used to practise levitation, lying face down and concentrating with such hypnotic intensity that I persuaded myself I was floating an inch or two off the floor. My memories of having drifted like a toy balloon around the ceiling of my bedroom, and of having glided down the long sloping field below the school, were convincingly vivid, but a ballast of scepticism kept me from telling anyone of them. Rapturous cloud-explorations, snipelike towerings, angelic freefalls, reoccurred for many years thereafter and are among my most treasured unrealities.

'Hushaby baby in the treetop, when the wind blows the cradle does rock' was not among the mantras of my childhood, but hearing it now reminds me of early fantasies of being born in a bird's nest high among branches swaying in the wind. Perhaps that balancing, flexing, world promised a strange security. My father, who knew about such things from his own treeclimbing, bird's-nesting, boyhood, often told me, as a marvel, how the woodpigeon's eggs lie safely on a mere half-dozen crossed twigs. As for the moment of terror 'when the bough breaks', I had already survived it, for once when I was no bigger than a monkey a branch snapped off under my weight, and I fell rather slowly to earth astride its thick, air-resisting, foliage. I was good in trees, showing off to all who would pause to admire how I could hang by my knees, and daily practising Tarzan-swings from branch to branch of a long-suffering tree known as the Coronation Oak in a little park near home. A few years ago, when I visited the deserted villages of the Anasasi Indians built into hollows of a cliff hundreds of feet above the canyon floor of the Mesa Verde, I found myself envying the children who had looked down like hawks' nestlings at the maplike geography of their future hunting grounds. But I am not a cliff-climber; the cliff-edge is the controlling emblem of my life, as I hope to explain deeper into this book, and I do not transgress it.

Once, after I had waited many hours for a lift by a road that was evidently little travelled, in Norway, an eagle appeared high overhead. Two crows from a nearby wood set out to pester it into quitting their patch of sky. Was it really in their territory according to bird-law? As they laboured upwards for minute after minute, shrinking to ragged dots almost lost against the pale glare, I began to have a sense of how far up the eagle was. It was only with great effort that the crows reached its level, whereupon it flapped one huge wing at them as if shaking dust off a carpet, and sailed out of range of harassment. Height, then, can only be won with expense of energy; the vertical dimension is not as easily penetrable as the horizontal ones; flight-space is stratified by increasing difficulty; up-draughts, thermals, are winds that help one up invisible hills.

Questions of how the spaces of experience, human and non-human, relate to real space, whether they can always be expressed as colorations, tensions, deformations or indexings of it, and whether real space itself is a perpetual creativity beyond comprehension in terms of the conceptual spaces of geometry, have always intrigued me, and I am far from answers to such problems. I suspect that the impossibility of my dream-flights does not lie in their effortlessness but in some geometrical incoherence in the space they traverse; dreams can benefit from the logic of contradictory foundations, in that anything can obtain in them, if only because their contradictions are not attended to. (The dream contains only what is attended to by the dreamer.) But when their spaces are inscribed in real space, they can fall to earth.

I painted a number of works called 'Falling Bird' once. This was in Vienna in the mid-sixties; that lugubrious Cold-War city seems in fact to have called forth macabre and surreal expressions of several themes that happily have also surfaced in less phobic periods of my life. Some of these birds looked as if they had been falling so long they were reduced to desiccated anatomies. What had stopped them in mid-flight was not to be known from the paintings; it might have been a burst of radiation from the Armageddon we half expected daily at that time. Contorted, rigid, they fell through layers of grey vapour, or hung like black silhouettes against it as if seen by one in free fall alongside them. Insensible or indifferent to all other influences, they were abandoned to gravity. That supreme space-shaper, the commanding force orthogonal to all the tentative, laterally spreading, webs of my mapwork, is immanent in much of what I have drawn or written.

A bird's flight-world is perfused by its song-world, a structure of intensely significant directions, distances, locations and regions, perceived through the influx of sounds made by its congeners and to a lesser extent by other species: warning cries tracking the prowl of a cat, nestlings' unappeasable demands, sexual advertisements, rivalrous bravado. We eavesdrop on this world, which intensifies both space and time for us: the echoing sea-cliff is redoubled by a peregrine falcon's gaunt clamour; a slothful summer afternoon is lulled into still deeper inertia by a woodpigeon's repetitious lucubrations. Stepping out of a cottage on the Aran Islands very early one spring day I found the slopes of rock and raggletaggle bushes around it being partitioned between half a dozen voluble cock blackbirds. Territoriality, the staking of exclusive claims, is the driving force behind much birdsong. What sounds like mere recreation is indeed re-creation: the reinvention or reimposition for another day of a political geography that had lapsed overnight. In fact a number of treaties were being drawn up as robins and wrens and other small birds added their distinctive signatures to that morning's crisp parchment. A superimposition of transparent maps, the brouhaha of languages in a cosmopolitan restaurant, the interweaving of games played by different age-groups of children in a school yard, are all inadequate images of the endless interpretability of space.

The various possible relationships between bird territories also remind me of those diagrams in textbooks of logic, in which, for instance, two overlapping circles or similarly simple shapes, standing for two sets of elements, divide the page into various parts representing those elements that are members of both sets, of neither, of one but not the other, and so on. These Venn diagrams (so called after their inventor) are also useful in the formal logic devised by Boole in the last century: the interior of a shape represents a proposition and its exterior the contradictory of that proposition; the overlap of two shapes represents the conjunction of two propositions. Such a structure of abstract argumentation is termed a calculus, from the Latin for a stone as used in reckoning. Just as propositions can be about propositions, so sets can have sets as their members – but these logical systems founder in self-contradiction if sets are permitted to be members of themselves or if propositions are allowed to refer to themselves, as Bertrand Russell proved. The successive catastrophes provoked in logic by Russell, Gödel and Turing suggest that thought is not a matter of piling up stones, for that gives no play for paradox. Some such train of associations, together with my abiding fascination with theories that lie just beyond my comprehension and like birdsong seem always about to crystallize into sense, motivated a deranged harangue I wrote a few years before that dawn chorus in Aran; it purports to be a lecture delivered by a man in a tree to an audience also perched in trees, in the University of the Woods:

Is thought a calculus? A calculus a stone? Thrown at a bird, let fall to sound a well, used in a wall against a wind? Admit the wind! To fence a field? Consider the territoriality of knowledge: the don defines a field (the territoriality of birds, we'll say), assumes a stance (his axiom: each bird sings only 'I am here!'), deploys his arms (poor scarecrow, the birds are flown already), and lets his field define himself. 'I am my place!' he sings, and produces proofs: 'The song's assurance dwindles with distance from the perch; each bird and its neighbour meet in equivocation and make their mutual boundary the locus of equal unconviction. Thus the land is parcelled out by blackbirds, thus by robins, thus by thrushes, in mutually invisible systems of exclusions ...' But Doctor Intelligence Discarnate views all from above, sees what is not to be seen (the crow's border crossing the wren's domain, linnetdom within chaffinchshire), discovers his hard calculus to hand and with it guards his empty coverts. Logic, not Song, is ritual attack! (Song is the riddle that turns upon itself.) If you are your thesis, best perfect its defences, claim complete originality, disguise guilty inclusions, defend your bounds against encroachment. For above all else you fear encirclement, the hell of being understood, analysed, part refuted, part absorbed and reinterpreted within a greater whole in which a fragmentary occluded you lives on, forced to chime its thinking with another's. Are you the defect in your objectivity, the vulnerable centre? Should you exclude yourself, renounce your place in the winged flux, become impenetrable, a stone, at rest in the safety of complete disjunction from your kind?

Turn, Professor! Seek the glimmerings of sense in the thickets of your theory. There is a pool in which you figure, ringed by fleeting diagrams of your inconsequential algebras. This structure of fears you think of as yourself reflects you well – and so the affronted incalculable outwits you! Self-description is the cuckoo's egg of contradiction among your sterile clutch of theorems – and an unexpected proof of kinship with the birds! From a con-

tradiction all things follow; it is the all-devouring foster-child that bursts apart your systems and teaches you to fly. Follow its derisive voice, poor pipit, beyond the circles of your Boolean mind! Become insatiate of possibilities, watch Venn's amoebae spiral out in unbelievable evolutions: multimen with flocks of voices, wind-tossed clouds of faculties and appetites juggled by perspective into momentary beings, infinities of selves lovingly nested one within another ...

So, crazed by mad analogies of sanities yet to be invented, the sad professor mounts St Francis's pulpit, humbly resolved to speak only as a bird speaks, for the pleasure of hearing a like voice return. And when the sun sets in his mind, as now, his thought flies inwards to its own dark woods, leaving a silence where it sang.

Rereading, I see an element of self-caricature. Perhaps the present book needs some apologetic preface; let this be it. I have written about many matters I do not understand (but if I restricted myself to what I do understand I would be wordless). Sometimes I have followed the sounds of words, trusting them (as a writer does; it is the difference between a writer and an intellectual) to lead me into sense. But I do believe that all things are in principle comprehensible – except two: the existence of the universe, and one's own existence. These are mysteries, in the sense that one cannot even frame a question about them. About the universe, 'Why?' just directs us back into the web of interconnections constituting it; about oneself, 'Why here? Why now?' is empty, as asked by an embodied here-and-now. Questions of how consciousness arises in nature, and how and what one consciousness can know of others, are proper, if intractable; humanity has been grinding away at them for thousands of years and has sharpened them, at least. But a mystery is a questionmark in search of a question; it is unappeasable.

The essays in this book hover, fascinated, about the self-mystery, and feel the wind of the universal mystery. They are all on themes, to do with space, that have outcropped often enough in my life – as a student of nature, of geometry, as artist, cartographer, topographical writer, environmentalist, hitchhiker, home-lover and cosmology-fan – to give it some continuity, at least in retrospective reconstruction. But they do not add up to an autobiography, a project that would not interest me; so far as my life-story goes, these are walks on the bank of a river of untold tales.

THE CURVATURE OF THE EARTH

The World Seen Edgeways

Horizons are the eye's best attempts upon infinity; we scan them avidly as if desperate to see as far as possible or searching for escape through the threadlike gap between the impenetrable globe and the indefinite depths of the sky. Perhaps two puzzles, one explicable and the other inexplicable, condensed into the mystique of horizons for me in childhood.

First, the rules of perspective, which I grasped at an early age. My parents were gratifyingly impressed by a drawing I did when about eight, of the undersides of the diningroom table and chairs seen obliquely from where I lay on the carpet – a worm's-eye view, they told me. The trick of drawing in perspective is to imagine that one has a single, cyclopean, eye, keep it fixed in position, mentally reduce the edges of things so viewed to a flat array of angles and intersections, and copy that onto paper. The result is nothing like the world as registered by two eyes set in a mobile head and backed by an interpretative brain, but it is curiously convincing. In a sketchbook mainly of childish scenes of interplanetary war, piously preserved by my parents, I find a little diagram evidently drawn to convince myself of the fact that an object subtends a smaller and smaller angle at the eye as it is removed farther and farther, and that, taken far enough away, it disappears. I used to like demonstrating this with drawings of roads winding away over rolling hills into the distance, vanishing into valleys and reappearing as ever-narrowing strips, until their two sides converged to a point on the horizon. I remember that a primary-school friend thought these drawings absurd; roads kept the same width all the way, he insisted.

The other puzzle was that of parallel lines meeting at infinity. (The unworldliness of the consideration suggests I was told of it by my uncle Richan, a quiet, unassuming Scot, my mother's brother and regarded with irritation by her because of his lack of initiative, who read Sir James Jeans and Baudelaire and did his best with limited talents to make a living as an artist.) Since parallel lines are chiefly famous for never meeting, this meant that anything and everything might meet at infinity, which therefore I could draw as a menagerie of whatever I was capable of drawing. Since I particularly liked drawing elephants, I made many pictures of parallel lines arrowing in from all directions, with constellations of elephants big and little.

The horizon, then, is where the possible and the impossible meet. Did it also impress me as an all-encircling threat? For otherwise I cannot account for a painting from my mid-teens, called 'A Man Cut in Half by the Horizon'. The man staggers towards one with terrifying or terrified hands raised above his head; his midriff is missing and in the gap one sees the dwindling road behind him and a low horizon between desolate heath and a lurid sky. Splashes of dark red along the roadside perhaps owe more to my defective colour-sense than to thoughts of blood. I showed this work to the physics master of the small provincial grammar school I attended. Why him, of all people, the representative of a version of reality compounded from blackboard-chalk and stale pipe-smoke, in the dragging gravity of which the school clock ran slow, who for year after year had reduced all the fantastic and precise 'Properties of Matter' to half a dozen experiments of mortal tediousness and indefinite outcomes? If I wanted to shock him I did not succeed. Instead of fulminating over the impossibilities of my scene, he merely asked why I didn't paint something beautiful, such as a sunset; nobody, he said, could even imagine a painting called 'The Ugly Sunset'.

That grammar school was in Ilkley, Yorkshire; the horizon of my fantasy was the skyline of the plateau above the picturesque crags and winding walks of Ilkley Moor itself. It is one of the Pennines' dark moorlands underlain by millstone grit; the next, north of it, is Emily Brontë's, and then come heights of the more luminous grey of limestone. I spent much time up there, sometimes with my younger brother and his small friends whom I coerced into scouring miles of heather for elephant hawk moth or oak eggar caterpillars, or with schoolfriends of my own, looking for golden plover nests or trying to rediscover a shallow pond we named Swoopers' Tarn because we were once driven off from it by diving seagulls and which lay in such a level expanse of bog that with our small statures it was difficult to locate from a distance, or alone, seeing the two gaunt pylons on the highest point of the moor – disused radio-masts from the war years, I think – as elementals, giant embodiments of nature's forces, stalking the edge of the world.

Cities were invented to protect us from the terrors and temptations of horizons. Façades stare down the would-be-wandering eye, direct it along perspectives that terminate in monuments to the centrality of the places they occupy. And the rebellious urge of some citizens – myself among them – to overcome these constrictions drives us to the tops of whatever poor heights the city's bounds enclose. In London my urge to drink space and inhale distance had to be content with the views from Hampstead Heath and Parliament Hill. Constable could look out of London from there, into the countryside beyond, but now it is impossible to see the city whole. Nor do these views have anything of the map about them; they reveal neither the grand theorems scored by the Enlightenment nor the knots left in the grain of the modern city by the medieval villages it has grown around. The subject may occupy 180 degrees or more of the visual field horizontally, but hardly five degrees from top to bottom; we see the city edgeways on, an expanse almost without volume, a crust.

Pining for horizons, I used to walk through London so far as possible as if I were in open countryside. The site of my 'University of the Woods' could have been Hampstead Heath, but was in fact, or in imagination at any rate, a scruffy bit of parkland by the Welsh Harp reservoir, beyond Cricklewood and Neasden – beyond, that is, from the point of view of West Hampstead, my village when that piece of fiction was written – across which I used to ramble, until the body of a youngster from a delinquent family we knew of was dug up there, and it no longer seemed a safe landfall from the sea of chaos growling all around it. From that (quite properly) modest eminence one sees the Greater London of dingy towerblocks, cardboard-box industrial units and turbid rivers of traffic, with enough aircraft overhead to define a loose skein of flight-paths hanging above and declining into it at various grey points of the compass. Some notes have surfaced, of my first expeditions there:

19/5/72 *I saw across the Kilburn valley (Watling St.) the spire of another church – from there one could look back and see the spire of the Priory Rd. church. Walking along Willesden Lane, 'I'll walk as far as the next village and then get the bus back.' And it is a village. In the dental lab window: 'Why not get an 18 or 22 carat gold tooth fitted to your dentures?' Front doors with names and numbers stacked against the wall in the scrap metal yard; mercury 14s. a lb. today. Mr Whisker next to the pet shop. Petropolis, a magnificent green and red perspex service station.*

I asked somebody 'What's that big building on the horizon?' He stared along the sideroad. His first horizon in London? 'Maybe one of those factories on the North Circular.' Later I found it is the GPO Research Centre. The parkkeeper in Gladstone Park identified Wembley Stadium for me; 'Cup Finals, we hear the roar.'

Beyond that, another valley, then up Dollis Hill. Dodging around to see the Adelaide Rd. towerblocks between the trees of Gladstone Park. Navigating by the sun through slow curves of semi-detached houses towards Willesden Green. A brilliant shortcut along Charlesworth Rd. Places you can see across London: from railway bridges, along the lines.

6/6/72 *Drizzle and semis to Gladstone Park, and a steep hill to the GPO Research Centre, but from there a great vista down and across the Welsh Harp (at last!). From the North Circular Road see church and rounded treetops of a clearly defined village on the other shore beyond the masts of sailing boats. On the south shore, along Blackbird Hill to Neasden. Long detour to get down to the northern shore. Little woods. A squeaking and rustling; waited, saw a little shrew (W.H. Hudson writes about this in* A Shepherd's Life*). Further on in the fields watched a pair* *of kestrels divebombing a crows' nest. The crows frightened, silent, crouching on the nest. One flew off across the fields and was almost beaten to the ground by the hawk swooping on it. Ambiguous end; did both crows leave the nest? The other kestrel sat in the field for a long time. A robin perched a yard or two from me as I watched all this; thin wistful song, a lonely bird.*

18/6/72 *Went back to see if in fact it was the crows which were robbing the kestrels' nest. Bus to Hendon Broadway; the sight of the lake is nearly as romantic as the inn-sign of it there, 'The Old Welsh Harp'. Squally day, grey and silver. Coots and ducks on the waves. Watched the nest for a long time, sheltered under an elm from the rain. A hawk came into the tree briefly; the only crows were a little group in the field 200 yards away. So it was the hawks nesting in an old crows' nest. The kestrels hovering and gliding across to the far side of the lake – and beyond them the regular sloping down of airliners towards Heathrow, quite silent at that distance, two visible at any time. A march-tit by the lake and yellow flags. An hour there, and no-one passed! Past the sailing clubs to Blackbird Hill, walked up it but couldn't get much sense of the land beyond. Bus back to Willesden Garage, took the wrong turning coming out of a little bookshop and got spectacularly lost. Arrived at the Harrow Road! and walked back to Willesden Lane by endless slow-curved avenues. It was the bus-ride that broke my contact with the land's directions.*

But in the modern city's layout 'the land's directions' have been overridden by the impetus of transport; it is perverse to identify oneself with the losing side, the buried past, in this historical *agon*. My 1960s artistic projects for bringing into consciousness London's suppressed geography – for instance, a walk along the course of the long-built-over Kilburn, the Kyle Burn of lost rural ways, leaving a bunch of watercress on the doorstep of each police station I passed – could be seen not only as whimsical but as life-denying. The city builds, tears down, rebuilds, its own horizons; its skylines burgeon and decay like the close-packed petals of a rose. For the truly London pastime of identifying from half-obscured profiles buildings with names and histories, Primrose Hill, on the verge of the inner city, is the place. I forget what exactly is underfoot at the highest point of that shallow dome of trim grass and treed walks, but it is worn down into hardness or concreted or tarmacked, as if the constant directing of attention away from it to the vistas below has somehow annulled it. I used to call it 'The Point of View' and identified it with the site of the foot of Jacob's ladder, and indeed it did occasionally reveal a visionary dimension to the city. One evening M and I were strolling on the slopes of the hill when we met a poet of our acquaintance coming down. He said, 'There's a lot of people up there; they must be expecting an event,' and went on his way hunched in introspection. We hurried up to join the gathering on the Point of View. Nothing was happening but the evening itself; the event was London's bewitchment by the level rays of sunset, its transformation into a poet's city, Samarkand, Xanadu.

Lines of Latitude

Flying across the Great Plains, say from New Orleans to Denver, one looks down at a flatland divided precisely into squares, most of them further divided into four. Many of these smaller lots contain a huge circle, the extent of a crop irrigated by sprays on a centrally pivoted, slowly rotating beam; anyone seeing these discs for the first time will think, as I did, of a giant game of draughts played on an endless board. Underlying and half-effaced by this modern, rectilinear, rule-bound geography is another, vague, senescent, of sprawling elevations that look too slight to be captured in contours, and meandering streambeds abandoned to stagnancy and evaporation. If nature seems to be wandering at a loss in a directionless expanse, the work of humans knows the cardinal points of the compass exactly, and the roads that follow and define the boundaries of lots are singlemindedly intent on getting out of here, wherever 'here' is, as directly as possible. As the shadow of the plane advances over it for hour after hour, the agricultural geometry at last begins to lose conviction, the succession of squares wears out, a subdued chaos of desert shows through. Eventually only a few highways persist in their monomaniac westward career towards the Rockies.

Westward is the warp-direction, the underlying and sustaining drive of ruthless purpose, in this awe-inspiring tapestry of the advance of the frontiers of cultivation. A thousand miles of Euclid might also appear to be a convincing demonstration of the flatness of the Earth, the potentially limitless extent of human domination, but on reflection the grand theorem of the Plains proves just the opposite. While Manifest Destiny is obviously responsible for the general westwards trend of this landscape, why is it in fact orientated so precisely east-west? Could it not have run towards the west-north-west, for example, or in whatever other direction historical contingencies might have aimed it initially? In laying out such a uniform schema, the ideal would be for at least one set of boundaries to be straight and parallel, i.e. to maintain a constant compass-bearing and a constant lateral separation. But a line that intersects the meridians at any fixed angle other than ninety degrees will wind around the globe and if prolonged will eventually spiral in towards one of the Poles; therefore another line starting at a given separation from it and following the same compass-course will ultimately converge with it, and the strip of land between them will taper to nothing. On a continental scale, the only way to avoid the convergence of loxodromes, as such lines of constant bearing are called, is to have them running exactly east-west. Thus the claim of human sovereignty over the land, so aggressively asserted by this whole vast system of subdivision, is subverted by its prime parameter, forced into a covert assent to the curvature of the Earth and the finitude of our dominion.

From similar causes arise the complexes of feelings we invest in elements of the scaffolding of latitude and longitude: the Poles, the Meridian of Greenwich, the Equator, the Arctic and Antarctic Circles; these (always capitalized) intangibles combine totalitarian presumption with a due recognition of littleness. I have no experience of the Equator, and wonder at the demeaning horseplay associated with the crossing of it; but I have paid my respects to the Arctic Circle, the latitude at which on midsummer's eve the sun's apparent course is a circle that just touches the horizon, or would, in a perfectly spherical world of ideal horizons.

It was a Sunday; after many hours standing by the empty road to the deep north of Norway, I was offered a lift by a young would-be playboy in an open sportscar, driving to nowhere in particular because of what he described as 'the small opportunities' of the little town he was employed in. He was delighted to take me as far as I wanted to go, and it was an exciting ride, breezing through sunshine and empty moorlands towards that abstract line stretched taut around the curve of the globe, which I could feel ahead of me like the tape at the finish of a footrace. When we saw pretty blonde girls picnicking we shrieked to a halt, and then, as they ignored us, roared off again. Eventually a small sign announced the Arctic Circle. We stopped where a few cars were parked outside a little souvenir shop, stretched ourselves in the sunshine, jumped across the line drawn on the road, and poked about among dwarf willow and reindeer moss for a while, in a wide barrenness that lifted snowy wings to the blue sky on either side.

My driver turned back from there, and I pressed on, determined to see the midnight sun from the best possible vantage point on the upcoming midsummer's eve. By stages and small adventures I came to a little port, and took a ferry to the Lofoten Islands. The sea was like black glass; the boat drew a lace curtain across it. The land of snowy peaks we were leaving, pale against a pale sky, followed us as wavering columns in the huge fan of the bow-wave. Silently another wall of rock approached, and opened a little to let us into a landlocked bay. A small town there was spread like fingers between immediate crags, and faced east. I determined to cross to the island's north-Atlantic outlook, and out of a certain obstinacy persisted in doing this by hitchhiking. I remember waiting a long time and with growing alarm to be lifted out of a desolation among needle-sharp peaks, where viciously screeching terns zipped to and fro over the surface of a fjord; I wondered if the fish were aware of these flying knives and forks above their two-way mirror ceiling. It was late in the evening when I was dropped off in a run-down fishing village. The family who had brought me on the last stage had evident misgivings about leaving me there.

Nobody was visible in the street, so I began knocking on doors, and after several enquiries learned that none of the houses kept visitors. The sun was still high and I could have slept out, but a bank of fog moving into the bay like a huge battleship looked ominous, and I was relieved when another door opened and a cheery old salt came out to survey me. We had no common language, but my needs were obvious, and without a word he stuck his pipe in his mouth, put me into a car and drove me down to the waterfront, and then beyond it. I already had a fine sense of arrival, of having gone as far as possible to greet the midnight sun from the edge of the inhabited world, but now I was amazed to find myself crossing a long rough causeway to an islet even nearer that ideal horizon. It was scarcely more than a large rock with a couple of gaunt sheds, in one of which was a room perched over the water's edge and reached by a ladder. The room was quite bare and smelled strongly of fish, but there were bunks, and two little windows looking at the sun. I had no food apart from an apple and a lump of goat's cheese I had already dined and breakfasted off several times because the few shops and restaurants of the region had been closed by the time I reached habitation each evening and were still closed when I left in the mornings, but drinking water was to be had from a hose in the deserted fish factory close by. There my benefactor left me. A hippie couple lurking in another room of the building told me it was used during the winter by cod-fishermen, who moored their boats below and snatched a few hours' rest from the waves in it without quite coming ashore. There was no one else on the islet. I was delighted with the extremity of my situation.

Towards midnight I wandered out among a few drifting scarves of fog. The sun, a pale disc, was gliding at a perceptible rate along the perfect skyline of a calm sea. Seabirds shrieked horribly. I looked for a memento of this mournful end of the world, but there was nothing on the rocks apart from a few bits of the sponge called Dead Man's Fingers. In the middle of the islet stood an enormous skeletal structure of wooden beams, a hundred yards long, shaped like a nave with side-aisles. It was hung with thousands of dried codfish, whose brown and twisted corpses gaped downwards. The stench was confounding. I had hoped some ceremony would suggest itself for this moment, but could not have foreseen that it would be staged in a temple of death. As the sun rolled along the horizon, I steeled myself to walk, processionally, through the appalling gibbet-cathedral.

The next day – but it was already the next day; I had just seen two days being arc-welded into one – I recrossed the island, heading home to my love in London. The ferry to the mainland sailed at 11 p.m.; at first the sun was hidden behind the mountains of the island, but when we drew out it appeared above them in a sea of pink feathers. From a few miles away the island chain was a long wall of peaks as sharp as the beaks and claws of the hungry birds that followed us, and dark blue against the rosy sky and the huge disc of the sun. As the islands shrank back I saw for the first time in my life how large the sun really is. The islands, the whole globe, could have dwindled to a dot, and the sun would still have looked the same size. At midnight it was at the lowest point of the vast slanting circle it makes round the sky, and the circle held the earth like a pebble in the palm of a hand.

BALLISTICS

Flat in long grass, I watch the bomber coming in low over the palm trees. As its bomb doors gape open I tilt my bren gun up and fire into the dark of its belly.... Battle is the shift and crisscross of death-lines in the hand of space; one is supposed to read them, lurk in their interstices, then run between or under or magnificently overleap them, to claim a vantage and reconfigure them. However, I had no bullets in my gun to bring the plane down in flames and whoever was in it had no bomb to smear me around the walls of a crater; the episode was a practice-run, a moment in a military exercise that swept over me in a mind-splitting roar and otherwise left me for long hours to contemplate ants crawling up grass stems. But it was a thrill, even if I had to smile at myself wrestling with my bren gun, which toppled over at the crucial moment; I was invincible, a solo hero, like the man in a war film I saw once who lobbed a stick of dynamite into the path of the fighter diving to strafe him, causing the plane to disintegrate satisfactorily in a whirl of black smoke.

Ballistic space, the space imposed by weapons of death-at-a-distance, with its fields of fire, possible and actual trajectories, its terrains denied and zones of security and danger, is a playground mankind exults in. Show a male child a gun, the sociobiologists say, and he climbs back up the spiral staircase of the genes to the African savannahs, where a million generations were spent killing animals with throwing-sticks; that was the age of the world in which the qualities of manliness were born, and ours is the age in which they have entered into a suicide pact with technology.

Not so, womankind. During the war my parents were living near a target of the Luftwaffe. When sirens howled in the night and Daddy went out in his bomb-proof ARP hat, my mother used to crouch beneath a great stone slab in the larder with us two children gathered under her (it was the most dangerous place in the house, but how was she to know?) and try to assure us that the forces thundering around us were all protective: 'Was that one of ours, Mummy?' we would crow whenever a bang shook the house, and she would wail, 'Yes! That was one of ours!'

As it happened, no bombs fell in our suburb and we children never saw the ugliness of war. Some mornings we were delighted to find trees and bushes hung with ribbons of aluminium foil, the chaff dropped by German bombers to confuse radar signals. Once when we had stolen away, unknown to our parents, to dig out spent bullets from a sandpit used by the Home Guard for target practice, we stirred up a puddle with some yellowish oily stuff in it, which suddenly exploded into a delightful momentary fountain. When Flying Fortresses began to be talked of by the adults, my imagination was fired and I made many drawings of winged castles that rose in battlements rimmed by cannon. The family moved to Ilkley shortly after VJ Day, and in subsequent years one of the ways in which I came to know the Moor was as a network of routes for crossing it under sniper fire: crawling through stands of bracken, worming along little watercourses, sprinting from the shelter of one boulder to the next. At that age my zest for life required an enemy to enliven the action; the War was in the past and I had missed it.

When I did find myself in a sort of war, as a National Serviceman in the RAF towards the end of the Malayan 'Emergency', I was inexcusably (so it seems to me now) unconcerned with its moral and political dimensions. The hothouse of adolescence, which had protected me from the tedium of my latter years in school, the savagery of Basic Training and the ice of a nine-month radar course in huts on the Wiltshire Downs, seemed to expand in Malaya to enclose a whole fervent world. The towers of cumulus pulsing with lightning all round the evening horizon, the exquisite girls who grouped themselves like bouquets and garlands of flowers in the streets or on the beach, the abyssal silences between gong-strokes in the Buddhist temple I haunted, the lurid backstreet nightlife to which fellow-conscripts less inhibited than I were keen to introduce me, all existed in the same perfumed atmosphere as my own rampant blooms of knowledge, desire, religion and poetry.

The malign aesthetics of weaponry took root in this tropical garden too. After some months spent puzzling into defective radar sets in the quiet of the servicing bay, I was banished to work on aircraft on the dispersal strip, where wing surfaces grew too hot to touch in the afternoons and one's shoulderblades made dents in the tarmac when one lay under the fuselage of a fighter. This was supposed to be punishment for arguing with the sergeant, who regarded me as lazy and insubordinate (whereas I was merely incompetent and distrait); but in fact I preferred the ferocious sunlight on the strip, the vigorous camaraderie, even the stinging blast from jets manoeuvring on the ground, to the torpid slacking of the bay. My letters home were rhapsodies:

... a much better life, spacious and turbulent with noise and movement, and full of hard angular facts, sun, wind and blue sky; a welcome relief from intellectual questionings. The expanse of sky is immense. Inland, mountains show far away over lines of dark green palm forests, and towards the sea runs the long air-strip, past the line of Canberras gleaming in the sun, past the control-tower, ending right on the beach. The sea shows through a last screen of curving palms, and immediately opposite rises Penang Island – paradise island – sunlit and forested hills behind the busy harbour, white houses showing around the top of Mount Pleasure (its actual name). One towering white cumulus cloud is invariably anchored there, trebling the height of the island, like a fantastic whorl of cream on a small cake. In the early morning the island's hills are banded with layers of mist and the guardian cloud rises majestically through white sheets of stratus. The first jet-engine wakes and breaks the ice of the morning silence, and a Venom roars along the runway to blast its way into the air, rising slowly against the mass of the island, banking and climbing over the shoulders of its hills to disappear into a sky no longer a blue ceiling but a palace of invisible corridors and stairs. All day there is a coming and going: groups of Venoms and Canberras perform endless evolutions and circuits above, Valettas and Dakotas, Hastings, Hermes and Argonauts arrive majestically, occasional odd specimens drop in and everyone stops work to argue their names – Beaufighters, Provosts, Doves, Pembrokes, Pioneers, Austers, wind-tossed Tiger Moths, immense Lincolns creeping down the sky and almost overshadowing the hangar, Bristol Freighters and Vampires.

The Canberra is one of the most beautiful man-made things I have seen. Eight of them stand in line here, crouched with their noses low, every contour taut and purposeful, rounded poised motionless bulk giving an appearance of weight and power almost belied by the slim long engines. They move down to the end of the runway in solemn whispering procession, and turn into position one by one. Each pauses for a few moments letting the engines rise to full power, then releases the brakes to slide slowly forward and accelerate steadily, until first the nose and then the wing-wheels leave the ground as it streaks past our dispersal-strip. At that climactic moment the engines are battering the air with a rich bellying thunder, a gamut of sound from a thin speed-whisper to great dark waves of din shuddering the ground and gripping the buildings with giant hands, undertones of savagery and war. The power and the menace die to distant thunder and grumble over the horizon, the still clouds reaffirm silence, the heat nails sound to the earth. Then the Canberra returns, power sublimated into speed, swooping silently towards us and breaking into a great climbing turn sliding easily over the sky as the shriek hits us like a wave breaking on the shore. What a bomber, to climb more steeply and manoeuvre more adroitly, fly faster and higher than any fighter! One sees why they carry no guns!

What more could the heart desire – a finer ballet in a more romantic setting?...

But what was it about, this savage parade? The elusive Chin Peng lurked somewhere in Malaya or over the border in Thailand; we were not told why his terrorist bands had to be exterminated or what they were fighting for, nor did we ask. Only once did I see the planes taking off in anger, as it were:

Worked all Saturday from 5.30 am to 5.30 pm, all for some terrorists causing trouble down south. I remember loading rockets by yellow moonlight before dawn, and the Canberras and Venoms taking off at first light (Can-

berras climbing implacably, black against the green-grey eastern sky, each trailing two long wavering streamers of vapour). And at midday bombs, and in the afternoon, when we were tired and our eyes beginning to feel gritty and there was an awful clarity of light under the metallic heat of the sun, we were battering open boxes and hauling out the long heavy chains of ammunition for the cannon; beautiful things to handle, each bullet about 8" long with bright brass and black enamel, richly glittering weighty ropes of them. Snatching meals while the planes were out on each strike, hurrying to meet them when they came in and rectify any snags and unload and reload etc. And what a day for the poor bandits. They ambushed an Aussy patrol in the morning and killed three, and lost two men in the ensuing battle, and then our strikes were mounted in an immediate follow-up (these are the only times their positions are known for bombing, when they meet a patrol like that). So they were chivvied through the jungle with bombs bursting and rockets shrieking and Venoms diving with their automatic cannon pumping bullets at the treetops, and finally (in theory) into the arms of encircling patrols. All five of them, no doubt.

In general we knew, or thought we knew, that such sorties did no good and no harm, that these thousands of missiles would fall into the forest and be buried in leafmould. It was said that the rockets the Venoms carried were too crude to hit a target, but that the noise they made in smashing through trees was effective in demoralizing the enemy. Perhaps we accepted such opinions as palliatives to our consciences; certainly we felt no ill-will towards the jungle shades. The reasons for the Emergency, its dark roots forking and reforking down through the Independence Movement and the resistance under Japanese occupation, into the long imperial past, were sometimes discussed in the circle of expatriates and local intellectuals I came to frequent, but I never joined in, aware of my ignorance and obsessed by internal debate as I was. Often I visited the temple of Ayer Itam on the island, heard the gongs, 'so slow that every stroke seemed the last, a draining of the blood out of the world', contemplated the house-high nut-brown Teaching Buddha sitting with raised hand behind threads of incense rising from joss-sticks. Once I brought one of those 'hard angular facts' learned on the strip to him, but 'he just sat there and, as always, said nothing'.

He might have told me the reason for this*: On Thursday the Venoms went on rocket practice. Early in the morning a tractor towed onto the strip a train of low trolleys stacked with rockets – heavy cylinders about 6' across and 1'6" long, of concrete (for practice purposes) backed by a metal tube about 4' long crudely finned at the tail. These were loaded onto the fighters, two or four under each wing, close by the fuselage. The planes trouped off, and came back at odd times of the day. A few came back at lunchtime when I was standing by. One of them for some reason had not fired its rockets. I went out to ask the pilot of the plane next to it how the wireless had behaved. As I approached him there was an explosion and a great rushing noise like a continued explosion from the other plane and a rocket cut a groove across the tarmac, hit a lump at the edge and I watched its trajectory high over the palm trees some 150 yards away. Behind the plane a man was lying on his back where he had been thrown from working on the rockets under the wing; his forearm stood up in the air oddly. Someone was running and shrieking 'Ambulance!' and someone else was crouched whimpering; everyone was running and calling; then they stopped, and someone brought a sheet of canvas, because he was dead....*

In reading through these diary-like letters (carefully dated and preserved in order by my mother and now, after her death, returned to me as if finally deemed undeliverable) I notice certain tactful omissions and elisions, and I wonder why I worried her with this episode, which I had to follow up with assurances that such accidents happened extremely rarely and that I was in no danger. However, two subjective details of the event did remain unmentioned, and have often resurfaced in my thoughts. First, while all that commotion was taking place – and it was over in a few moments – I was following the rocket's flight with my eye. Though aware of the sudden vortex of distress off to one side of me, and the death at its still centre, I was fixated on the great leap and distant fall of the inert lump of concrete and metal, as if testimony to the perfection of its parabolic arc would be required of me. And secondly, and hardly more than a second later, finding myself face to face with the young pilot officer I was about to salute, who had just stepped out of the cockpit and still wore the gaunt marks of his oxygen mask on his cheeks, I asked him about the wireless, as if it were of prime importance to hold to the procedures of normality. He looked at me astonished, then said politely that the wireless was in order. He might even have been grateful; a crevasse in time had opened before us, I had stepped across, he had followed, and it had closed again behind us. In fact we had all got across it in one way or another, except for the lad who died.

A CAREER IN ART

Right Hand

Miss Heaps, a sweet-tempered bun-shaped Ilkley lady, was my first art teacher. Side by side at the easel in her cramped little front room we worked on pastel copies of Van Dyck's 'King Charles the First', paying special attention to reflections in the armour, and of portrait photographs of cats and dogs, in which she would make one gleaming, lifelike eye, and I would make the other. Soon thereafter I became a modernist, and have remained one since. I attribute this to the art master of the local grammar school, Tommy Walker, who differed from the drab gaolers in charge of other cells of the curriculum in that he would smuggle in evidences of an outer world of creativity, not ongoing in Ilkley, perhaps, but not impossibly far removed. I remember his delight in *Under Milk Wood*, which he spent an entire afternoon reading to the class when it was first published. But what was modernism? Answers were as hard to come by and difficult of interpretation as information about sex. Somewhere I read an article which laid it down that Sickert's 'Ennui' was a truly modern painting, and I spent a lot of time poring over a small and blurred reproduction of it, trying to make out this quality of modernity. Herbert Read's book *Art Now* was subjected to deep looking too, and I took his various exemplars so deeply to heart that even nowadays when I come across one of the peculiar works he plucked from nonentity, such as Edgard Tytgat's 'Springtime' in the art museum in Brussels, I hail it as an icon of culture on a flight with the Winged Victory of Samothrace.

From such reading I gathered that the eternal enemy of art was 'The Academy', and that in each young generation the only artists worthy of respect were those disapproved of by the preceding generation. Art could not be taught; the ecstasies of creativity were the reward for selfless endurance of neglect and rejection. Art schools, I deduced, would be staffed by today's equivalents of those dullard painters and sculptors who figure in art history only in the blazing light of the pupils who rebelled against them. Science was different; discovery there was a matter of standing 'on the shoulders of giants' rather than striding across the fallen bodies of pygmies. Since I wanted both sorts of glory, I would study maths at university, and paint untutored.

My paintings of adolescent years varied from a depressive realism to a tortured expressionism, but always with a stiffening of the 'formal relations' I read about in R.H. Wilensky's *The Modern Movement in Art*. By my first year at Cambridge I had a style of my own, or rather two styles impacted and superimposed one on the other, in which flame- or leaf-like shapes were constrained by and played against a Mondrianesque rectilinear grid. Perhaps in a few examples these fraught contradictions achieved a tolerable outcome; at any rate one of them, exhibited in Heffer's Gallery, caught the eye of an art-loving mathematics lecturer, who wrote me a note about it. Some time later – it must have been after the exams at the end of my second year – I had the idea of starting a picture-lending scheme in my college (which I had decided was a philistine hole dominated by self-satisfied lawyers), and I called on this lecturer for advice, knowing that he had done something similar in his own college. He greeted me with 'Congratulations! You got a Second.' It had not occurred to me that he would be involved in marking papers. 'What sort of a Second?' I asked. 'The last one,' he said, and showed me a list of names in which mine actually stood two places below the cut-off line for second-class degrees, but was bracketed and furnished with an arrow that looped around and reinserted it just above the line. I was not bold enough to ask the reason for this miraculous assumption, which I suspect was a tribute to my artistic rather than my mathematical talents. A stern letter from my college followed me home that summer, warning that greater application would be necessary if I was to avoid sinking to a third-class degree in my final exams. Indeed, given the amount of time lost in my Cambridge years to drawing whimsical cartoons for the newspaper *Varsity*, designing incompetent layouts for undergraduate journals such as *Granta* and *Gemini*, scene-painting for the Amateur Dramatic Company, and other artistic activities I soon came to look back on with embarrassment, I was lucky to achieve a Second in the end. Fortunately I was blessed with a groatsworth of geometrical wit at the crucial moment in my finals, and perhaps that result was achieved despite, rather than because of, my aesthetic endeavours.

It was still to be some years before I would define myself as a painter; travel was my priority, and for that I needed a job. I was keen to revisit the East, of which my National Service had given me a taste; the names of Sumatra and other Conrad-attested fragments of Orient rang in my head. I had an interview with Shell during my last term, in the course of which I happened to mention that oil installations had spoiled the vista of the Straits of Malacca from Singapore Hill, whereupon the interviewer suddenly remembered that Shell didn't need any more mathematicians. My tutor tried to elucidate my ambitions and set me off on a career. By elimination, teaching had become my vocation, and since I was frightened by the thought of facing a class of youngsters, I wondered if my speciality was to be Adult Education. Gently he gave it as his opinion that I 'would find Adult Education in Borneo to be something of a Chimaera or Will-o'-the Wisp'. Next, I responded to an advertisement from an American institution, Robert College, on the Bosphorus. The golden grime of Istanbul had enraptured me on a vacation trip the previous summer; Turkey would be Orient enough. And as the Americans were desperately in need of a maths teacher for the Academy that prepared Turkish boys for college entry, and would start paying straight away, all was soon arranged, and we (I had paired with M by then) set off on a leisurely progress to Istanbul via Athens, with diversions to Mykonos and Delos. It was the beginning of three Aegean-centred years.

Squally weather, especially the first of those years, what with my inexperience in class and the coups and curfews attending the fall of the Menderes regime, and artistically a mere groping in dark and dazzle towards my final commitment to being a painter. In the paintings I produced, mostly after Saturday midnights, the conflictual schema of my Cambridge works reappeared in the guise of ancient masonry prised apart and held together by sinewy vegetation – a trace of my ocular feastings in Mycenae, Olympia,

Delphi, Naxos, and in the sumptuous decay of Istanbul itself. After an initial immersion in the hard-partying campus life of Robert College, we tended to withdraw from it and found our friends among the artists of the city, in a little Bohemia whose aesthetic loyalty was to Paris rather than to the wolf-grey Turkey of Atatürk or to the faded tatters of Ottoman splendour some of them had inherited.

Mehmet was the most flamboyant of these latter. His apartment, up five cavernous flights of stairs in old Pera, was a museum in meltdown; on one visit we found him bundling up the uniforms of two of his ancestors, a Vizier and a Grand Vizier, and had our photographs taken in them before they were carried off to the pawnshop. Mehmet was tall, handsome in a raffish way, dressed with a nautical air, and almost as thin as the knife-blade figures he used to paint on seven-foot-long planks. His wife, Sevim, was the most beautiful girl I've seen or imagined; her beauty was a physical shock, and once when I introduced her to a colleague from the college at a party I saw him turn white, then green, then red, as perhaps I had myself on first meeting her. But Mehmet was a drinker and a philanderer, recurrently in disgrace over one escapade or another, and on returning from an absence we were annoyed to find that he had been using our flat for one of his affairs. Like many Istanbul intellectuals, he eked out a living by translating French or English works into Turkish; he borrowed a copy of Malraux's *The Voices of Silence* that I'd treasured since my teens, and when we went to say goodbye to him and repossess the book before leaving Turkey for the last time we found that he had underlined passages throughout and let his infant son scrawl on its endpapers. In revenge we omitted to return a collection of records of modern music we had borrowed from him.

Two artists who became our friends were Omer Uluç, a *tachiste* whose canvases now seem to us to have prefigured the opaline cloudscapes of our Connemara windows, and Yüksel Arslan, a surrealist who lived below one of the great cemeteries that surround the old city like an exoskeleton. He used to collect the bones washed downhill to him by rainstorms and grind them up with honey and pigments to paint obscurely lurid little scenes in which one could make out half-formed grotesques goading each other with monstrous sexual prongs. Once when he and Omer were going off down the road after a merry dinner with us, I leaned out of our first-floor window and tossed Yüksel a small gift – an egg, as he discovered when he caught it. As a good surrealist he had to swallow his annoyance at being splattered by this *acte gratuite*. The thrown egg was something of an art-form for me at that period.

We formed a deeper attachment to the painter and printmaker Aliye Berger-Boronai. She was at first acquaintance a fright, with her yellow hair and strident make-up, feather boa and antique corset, but we came to love her delicately-boned face and hands and her deep, tragicomic eyes. Her seedily luxurious apartment, darkened by heavy curtains and crowded with canopied sofas, was dominated by a portrait which leaned out from the wall: a romantic violinist, all white brow and shirt-front, poetic locks, sweeping gesture with the bow – her dead husband, a Hungarian she had eloped with, and who had betrayed her; we often heard how she had hidden in a tree with the intention of shooting him and his mistress. Her family, with its palace connections, had been scandalized by her marriage. Once we visited their deserted house on Büyükada, an island in the Sea of Marmara favoured by Viziers as being out of reach of sudden summonses to the Palace, and where the Sultans used to pen their over-ambitious brothers. It was a huge, plain, dilapidated wooden building almost hidden in ivy, in a forlorn garden with a bare pergola and dried-up grotto. The main door led into a great vacant reception room with another grotto at the far end, a dusty tumble of dried-out rock-pools and waterfalls. Upstairs, room after empty room, long undisturbed except when Mehmet borrowed the house for his occasional drunken parties, and a boxroom stuffed with rotting documents in Arabic script. Aliye could remember the tedium of afternoons in this house, listening to her elders discussing politics over tea with a smartly dressed young officer, Mustafa Kemal, whose revolution would later ruin them and open the windows of Aliye's generation to the West.

In that new Turkey Aliye had won an art competition judged by Herbert Read, and she was an accomplished colourist; we have a large action-painting of hers, all spills and streaks of coloured inks, which have faded but still plumb galactic depths. I realized the acuity of her eye once when she stood on our balcony, which overlooked several miles of the Bosphorus edged by tiled village roofs and old sea-palaces of fretted wood, as busy as a street with ships and boats, and pointed out dozens of little patches of hues we hadn't distinguished, answering to each other across the water. Aliye gave me lessons in etching, and entertained us to glasses of tea brought up on a gimballed brass tray from a tea-shop in the courtyard below by a deaf old Armenian whom she paid with the flowers left by some previous visitor. Through her we were sometimes invited to 'kokteyls', openings of art shows, where we would find ourselves elbow-to-elbow with fabulous beings of another age – Balkis, reputed to have been Atatürk's last mistress, as rigidly curvaceous as a sea-horse, or Aliye's brother 'The Fisherman of Halicarnassus', stunning a chattering roomful into attention with the boom of the greeting he'd made fashionable, 'Merhaba!', and then mesmerizing us with a dithyramb about some girl in a white dress he'd seen: 'If I were so virginal, I would dispense virginities in hundreds, in millions!' The friendship with Aliye was one of the few we kept up after we left Istanbul for Vienna, where I arranged an exhibition for her; she arrived on the Orient Express, which was several hours late because the customs officers had been unable to penetrate the compartment entirely packed with framed canvases she had defended like a hawk on its nest. But for some reason I was impatient with her idiosyncrasies on that visit – 'How you have changed!' she said; 'You used to be so quiet, and now you're like fire!' – and thereafter we heard from her only occasionally and indirectly.

Perhaps I had changed; perhaps that is why I adopted my mother's maiden name Drever, instead of the prosaic Robinson, for artistic purposes at this time. Certainly after three years of teaching I knew what I wanted to do, which was to paint, and because of the disproportion between our American salaries and the Turkish cost of living, we had saved enough to fund the experiment for a while. Casting ourselves loose had its costs, though. After a summer's wandering in Dalmatia and northern Italy we arrived in Vienna in some psychic disarray, and rented a room in a dark, rambling apartment near the Opera. We found ourselves sharing a kitchen with two strange people. Nelly (short for Melpomene), a tall, angular Greek girl, belonged to a clique of free-floating young people, some of wealthy backgrounds, who seemed to have adopted evil and even suicide as a fashion accessory. She soon drifted out of our lives, but we became lastingly fond of Karl, the owner of the apartment, bizarre though his lifestyle was. A malnourished-looking, intense, dark-eyed youth from a poor farming background in Styria, he had two ambitions. One, for which he was already a few years too old, was to become a dancer with the Vienna State Opera. The other was to be kept by a rich elderly masochist. In despair over the first project, he would exclaim, 'For what I live in this last time?', and in explanation of the second, 'To have something a little lovely in my life!' (two formulae that have found a permanent home in our own speech patterns). The opera house, recently restored from bombed-out ruins to its original nineteenth-century pomp, dominated the quarter, in the perspective we learned from Karl. We would run down Bösendorferstrasse at the last moment to get standing-room tickets, and in the intervals mingle with the elegant on the cheap; sometimes we even gobbled a slice of Sachertörte and a glass of champagne in the crush and chryselephantine splendour of the bar, where we knew nobody and Evelyn Lear once gave me a magnificent look for staring at her admiringly.

But even the gilt ceilings of the opera house's public spaces had been shadowed by the horrible murder of a girlchild somewhere in the backstage labyrinths; the perpetrator was condemned to life imprisonment with the proviso that each year he spend the anniversary of his deed in darkness – a notion that might have figured in Musil's *The Man Without Qualities*. Despite all its brave resurrection of chandeliers from ashes, Vienna was macabre. Outside the charmed circle of the Ringstrasse, the most impressive monuments of the Vienna we now began to explore were not baroque churches and museums full of Austro-Hungarian loot, but Karl Marxhof and Friedrich Engelshof, long blocks of workers' flats with gun-slit windows, which had been shelled by the Dollfuss regime, and vast Hitlerite concrete air-raid shelters that still cast a grey-green gloom of defeat over certain streets. This unhappily historic city, so far from the touristic dream, no doubt had its say in the disturbed images I was producing at that time, which, I was further troubled to find, appealed to Nelly; 'torturous' was her term for them.

Even after we decided we had to insulate ourselves from Nelly's underworld, and had moved into an implacably bourgeois apartment in Sankt Elisabeth-Platz, Karl remained a friend and a source of the unexpected. He would drag us to a nightclub where he hoped to be allowed to stage a strip-show he had devised, in which a prostitute behind bars seduces the policeman in charge, to the screech and clang of *musique concrète* by Varèse (one of the records we had carried off from Mehmet, in fact). Once, he called with a pair of gloves for M which his dog had found in the street, and offered to teach her the 'Prinzess Striptease' (distinguished by the performer's keeping her gloves on to the last). Another time he invited us out with two cancan dancers, La Goulue and Valentin le Désossé, those rubbery icons of Toulouse-Lautrec's day, reincarnated as a cheery north-of-England couple; on the way home Valentin danced down the deserted street before us twining himself lovingly around lamp-posts. Although Karl never made it as a dancer he did find his rich masochist, and moved into his house for a while. But soon they quarrelled, Karl took off for America, there was a question of theft, and the police came to interview me about him; I suggested that there was no need to take him and his lover too seriously, but they politely informed me that they would decide what was to be taken seriously. We heard only once more from Karl after that; he was in San Francisco, where I am sure he has long since gone down into the furnace of AIDS.

Respectable as our new apartment was, with its great tiled stoves, the stained-glass in the bathroom door saying '*Teue Rechts und sheue Niemands*', and its pleasant outlook onto the market stalls and pretty church in the square, it had its sinister notes. There were bullet-scars in the masonry by the front doorsteps, and hidden behind the laurel bushes two inscriptions vividly reminded one of the history that had agonized around this very corner: a scrawl in German saying 'We will fight until we die', and a stencilled notice in Russian stating that the house had been searched and found free of arms. In this Cold War city unstably encamped on the ruins of its recent past, in which it was not done to ask anyone where they had been or how they had lived at any period in the previous thirty years, it was no wonder the already dark mood of my paintings took a turn into nightmare: atomic bombers flew in at the window, skeletalized birds fell through a lethal sky, monstrous creatures crawled in the sewers of towering 'cities in a vacuum'.

These works were very acceptable to the painters of the Wiener Schüle des Phantastischen Realismus, a group of belated surrealists under the enchantment of Bosch's nightmare-landscapes. I had my first exhibition in the gallery owned by the leading 'fantastic realist', Ernst Fuchs, a striking figure who might have been modelled on one of Durer's self-regarding portraits and whom we had occasionally glimpsed at the Opera accompanied by a Cranach Eve with waist-length golden ringlets. According to current legend he was subject to visitations from angels who periodically commanded him to chastity, and his minutely executed paintings revelled in a sex-haunted religiosity. Two of his emissaries called to vet my work for the exhibition and after examining the contents of my studio left with expressions of regard and admiration; later we found that one of my little sketchbooks of ink drawings was missing – a series of 'map-faces', which in the light of their absence now appear to me as the best of my work from that period. I don't remember that Galerie Fuchs succeeded in selling any of my paintings, but a review in the *Wiener Zeitung* praised my 'sleepwalking surefootedness', a phrase I have found comforting since.

Much of the sleepwalking mood of the city derived from the presumed omnipresence of spies. Vienna's artists were very given to *'Sezessionen'*, but if any two of them sat down at a café table to found a new group they were soon joined by two more, the spy from the East and the spy from the West; or so we were led to believe. One day we happened to notice a little plaque on the door of a grand building on the Ringstrasse: 'International Künstlerklub'. Enquiring within, we were warmly greeted, and soon found ourselves members, at a very modest fee, of a club that hosted evenings of wine and conversation in its pleasant old rooms; there was even talk of showing my work there. Later we were told by one of the members that the club was funded by the CIA through the Ford Foundation, with the object of seducing visiting Hungarian artists into defecting to the West; also that, having defected, with whatever good publicity for the cause of democracy this brought in its train, these artists soon discovered that there was no state support for them on offer, and quietly went home again. Similarly, the Galerie im Nansen-Haus, where I had my second exhibition, was said (by the same person) to have a connection with Radio Free Europe, proselytes of the Cold War. Were these things so? We would have had to turn spies ourselves to find out.

My best-attended exhibition in Vienna was an impromptu one, and an episode worthy of the city of Freud. The Council had decided that the attics of the city, stuffed with generations of junk, were a fire hazard, and decreed that on an allotted day each district should empty out all this repressed material onto the pavement for collection and disposal. When the day came for the first, the most fashionable and expensive, district to disburden itself, scavengers descended. Everything was analyzed meticulously; mounds of goods dwindled as metal spokes were snipped from old umbrellas and well-dressed ladies tottered away with antique standard lamps; in the end so much had found new homes that there was little for the authorities to remove. Then it was the turn of our district, and I took the opportunity of throwing out a stack of the worst of my paintings, most of them on hardboard. These attracted great interest. I spent the day leaning out of the window watching passers-by pulling them out of the heap, propping them up in a row, discussing them at length and going off with their selection under their arms. Towards evening a man arrived on a motorbike, gathered together the remainder and roared off, and then, mysteriously, half an hour later returned with them and carefully snapped each one across his knee before replacing it on the heap.

When it became clear that if I was to pursue the career of an artist it should be in a more challenging and future-oriented environment than this self-devouring city, we turned our minds to London. First I paid an exploratory visit, and called on some of the Bond Street galleries with a bundle of paintings and a letter from Herr Fuchs introducing me as a 'phantasmagorical artist'. One gallery owner studied the works for some time before announcing: 'You paint a world of which I want no part.' An official at the Arts Council counselled me to go away and study the paintings of Mark Vaux (whose abstractionism, as discreet as a bank-manager's suit, appealed to me then as little as it does now). Undiscouraged, we removed to London and found ourselves a flat in West Hampstead.

The year was 1964. The ascendancy of Pop Art concerned me as little as the other manifestations of Swinging London, but there was some intelligent painting on show that appealed to me (Bridget Riley, for instance, beginning her dazzling career), as my own work was reverting to the formal and abstract. One of my ongoing series 'The Dreams of Euclid' was accepted for the John Moores Biennial in Liverpool, a competitive exhibition that had established itself as a rite of passage for up-and-coming artists; the American critic Clement Greenberg was among the adjudicators and evidently set the tone that year. The painting attracted the notice of Guy Brett, art critic for *The Times*, and of Signals Gallery in Wigmore Street, London, which invited me to participate in a group show to be called 'Soundings 3'.

Signals was the standard-bearer for avant-garde work at that period. Paul Keeler (or his father, of the chain of opticians) supplied the money and David Medalla the inspiration. Medalla was a young Filipino 'elemental artist' whose career was already the subject of myth. His bubble-machines oozed mounds of foam, his bread-making machines excreted yards of dough, and his talk was so overwhelming that when he described his 'Homage to Kurt Schwitters', a collection of flying robots that had foraged over Japan and brought back their finds to his windowsill – a bus ticket, an article off a washing-line, etc. – which he then made into a collage, he convinced us momentarily that such a work existed. Among the artists hanging their work for the Soundings show I noted a man of sombre and reserved mien who seemed to hold himself at the same angle to the excited chatter as I did myself. His work, a thirty-two-foot-long painting constructed of ten or so panels in different colours, was by far the most distinguished contribution; 'a precise spectrum of cool summer', was how I described it later on. Peter Joseph became my closest friend and associate in the art world. Otherwise Signals was more loss than profit for me. Half an hour before the opening of that exhibition the artist Li Yuan-Chia decided to polish up a metal relief by Mary Martin that hung next to my paintings; he gave the can a good shake and it exploded; I came into the gallery at that moment to hear him screaming 'It's all right, Tim!' But the paintings were spotted all over, and I had to dash home and fetch replacements. After the show Medalla told me that a film company wanted to borrow my works to furnish a set; his mesmerizing babble left me with the flattering impression that the film was to be Antonioni's *Blow-up*, but in the event it turned out to be a romp with Max Wall, and the paintings were returned the worse for wear. Compensation – of a couple of hundred pounds – was agreed, but then Signals Gallery closed its doors unexpectedly in the way such galleries could be expected to do, Medalla and Paul Keeler vanished, and it took weeks of phonecalls to Mr Keeler Sr to explain the situation and exact my money. In all, Signals cost me a year's work.

Sometime later the Lisson Gallery was founded by Nicholas Logsdale and his partner Fiona, took on board several ex-Signals artists, and soon proved to be Signals' successor as shock-absorber of the new. Dashing around with cans of white paint, readying it for the opening exhibition, we almost persuaded ourselves it was an artists' co-operative venture. An idea in vogue at the time was that of the 'multiple', an artwork produced in large numbers of identical instances, forgoing both the Benjaminesque aura of the unique original blessed by the touch of the artist's hand, and the preciosity (and frequent fraudulence) of the 'numbered, limited, edition'. The concept was seen as a blow against the capitalist art world; economies of scale and industrial production processes would place these works in the financial reach of anyone who could afford a beer. My multiples were to be two prints in strip-cartoon format called 'The Theory and Practice of Dreams', in which little constellations of abstract shapes pursued an evolution of 'sleepwalking surefootedness' from frame to frame. They owed much to the technical diagrams I was drawing in the freelance-illustrator hours of my life that helped to keep us solvent at that period; in particular they were concocted out of the little symbols used in electrical and electronic circuit-design, available in sheets from Letraset.

Since money was need to print this 'unlimited edition', I wrote to Letraset Ltd explaining the ethics of the multiple and Letraset's role in this project, and asking for sponsorship. To my surprise the Chairman replied: he had never heard of multiples but would be happy to talk to me. I went down to their offices in Seven Dials, and found the Chairman to be in low spirits; he had been kicked upstairs, he explained, and missed the days when he was a young inventor taking on the world (like me, was the implication). He told me of the birth of Letraset: he was playing around with a sheet of transfers belonging to his children, and idly cut out the letters ILL in the backing film, exposing the ink layer within; then he pressed it onto a sheet of paper, rubbed the front, and behold, the lettering was imprinted on the paper. After that glorious moment, of course, years of research into inks were necessary and many financial disappointments had had to be endured before rub-down lettering became the world-wide industry it is today. So, he was sympathetic to my predicament, and called in his chief accountant to see what they could do for me.

The accountant studied the drawings for my 'Theory and Practice of Dreams' consideringly. Was it some sort of a puzzle game? On being told that it was art, he began a long sentence to the effect that while the company did acknowledge a certain limited obligation to fund artistic endeavours in the local community, my work was perhaps outside their remit ... whereupon the Chairman dismissed him rather shortly, and as soon as he had returned to his office phoned him and told him to make out a cheque for a hundred pounds to Timothy Drever. Thanks to this generous expression of fellow-feeling, I was able to have hundreds of copies of my abstract comic strips printed on good card. But then the fallacy of multiples, or at least of marketing them through the gallery system, became apparent: since they were to be so cheap, it was not worth anyone's while trying to sell them. Mine lay in the Lisson's print cabinets for some years until I was asked to remove them, and I have heaps of them in the attic to this day.

In those years when mass assembly seemed to be the art form most deeply concerned with great issues and our weekends were spent shouldering each other forward in Trafalgar Square and Grosvenor Square, watching the dreamers in Hyde Park give flowers to policemen, or suffering incomprehensible harangues on the Dialectics of Liberation in the Roundhouse, I frequently found myself caught up in the art-world's own little demonstrations. When the Conservative government was proposing to force the public galleries and museums to charge for entrance, a protest campaign was organized by a couple we knew who lived in a pop-art style flat, every surface densely covered in a collage of heterogeneous images, over the vegetable market in Camden.

They had hired a double-decker bus to tour the capital and advertise the cause, but before they had finished pop-arting the bus their spies tipped them off that Lord Eccles, the Minister for Art, was entertaining Princess Margaret to lunch at the Tate Gallery. Pamela phoned me, I dashed down to Camden where I found her hastily sticking shiny stars all over the interior of the bus, and with a few others we jumped in and careered off to confront the villain; one or two hopeful passengers hopped on at traffic lights and found themselves being whirled along for free, not necessarily to where they wanted to go. A number of reporters were staking out the Tate when we arrived and were hopeful that we would cause a row; a glamorous woman journalist well known at that period suddenly turned the rays of her charm on me – in fact I was tempted to tell her that the pupils of her eyes were like black saccharine tablets – but lost interest when it became clear I was not going to throw myself under the Princess's hooves. In the event the Minister emerged alone, a stately figure with the glow of a freshly cooked ham. We rushed up and informed him of our undying hostility to entrance fees and everything else he stood for; he remarked loftily that he had been collecting art before we were born, and departed unmoved and unedified.

Another rally, in the name of what cause I cannot now remember, also took place at the Tate Gallery. When I arrived a small knot of people in the windswept portico were trying to hold a discussion, the import of which was drowned by traffic noise. After a while I piped up with the suggestion that we might ask the Gallery to give us a room. They all turned round to see this new Robespierre suddenly arisen in their ranks. 'Great idea!' they said; 'You go and ask them!' So I marched in and politely put our request to the girl at the reception desk, and after a few minutes of disconcerted trotting to and fro behind the scenes a conciliatory, smiling, functionary appeared and led us to a distant and unfrequented gallery, where we sat on the floor for an hour or two and debated the perils of being 'absorbed by the System'.

Perhaps it was as an outcome of this occasion that a better-attended and officially tolerated meeting later took place in a conference room at the Tate. Gustav Metzger, a small, wizened and fragile-looking man with a shy little voice and, as I learned later on, an ego of iron, was among the speakers. (Gustav had fled to Britain from Hitler's Germany, found refuge as a gardener on the Harewood Estate in Yorkshire, and then in London attracted a degree of notice among the avant-garde for his 'auto-destructive art'.) His proposal for advancing our cause was that we should demand that the Tate exhibit a work by Gustav Metzger; I forget its nature but it involved huge piles of old newspapers he had accumulated over many years. Nobody was very interested in this suggestion and it did not come to a vote before we broke off for lunch. We drifted back from the cafeteria rather at our leisure; only four or five people were in the conference room when I came in, and Gustav, with the committee skills of a Lenin, was prevailing upon this 'quorum' to vote through his proposal. I was delegated to write to the Tate about it, and, dragged along by the democratic imperative, agreed to do so and actually had one or two sessions with Gustav drafting the letter, until reality broke through again and I abandoned the task.

Sometimes these meetings generated a moment of drama, a twinge of paranoia or spark of violence. I attended one in a London art school, where forty or fifty artists were assembled in a lecture hall to discuss our relevance or irrelevance to the affairs of the world. At one point of the tedious day I spent some time in a corridor outside the lecture room telling an art critic what an image of bureaucracy the conceptual artists were unwittingly projecting, with their filing cabinets of documentation and their printed notices directing one to do this or attend to that. Then I went to rejoin the main debate, and the instant I opened the door I heard Gustav cry out 'Tim! He's attacking me!' and saw him in the grips of a wild-looking young man, surrounded by apparently paralyzed observers. Having had no time to think, I was not paralyzed, and dashed to the rescue. Fortunately as soon as I grappled with him the wild man crumpled like a cardboard box and sat down apologetically, explaining that he was terrified of going to prison; it appeared that Gustav had been listing the names of those present, and this person had panicked at the thought that the list might fall into the hands of the police.

The only occasion on which I myself precipitated a jot of physical aggression was during one of Joseph Beuys's day-long performances at the Tate. On entering the gallery I found a dense throng at the far end of the main hall, with a disembodied, prophetic booming alternating with weedy squeakings arising from its midst. A disgusted leftist heading for the exit said to me: 'Beuys is in there explaining the Liberal Party manifesto!' By degrees I worked my way forward till I could see what was going on: a question-and-answer session, in which Beuys took care to retain control of the hand-held microphone, which he would point towards his interlocutor from a distance that made any voice but his own sound feeble. Two assistants on a platform were filming his every move. When I felt my hour had come, I stepped forward and held out my hand so purposefully for the microphone that he had to hand it over. I asked if he thought that every work of art implied a vision of society. That was a proposition he could hardly disagree with, given his own philosophy. I pointed out the impression of exclusion given by the present work of art (for these performances were supposed to be such), the wall of backs one encountered on entering. I can't remember his replies, but he was rattled, and at each interchange I made him give me back the microphone. I explained how oppressive it is to feel oneself part of someone else's work of art; I pressed on with uncharacteristically confrontational intent, until some more demonstrative radical than I was moved to leap into the arena, grab the microphone from Beuys and fling it aside crying 'Let's get rid of the technology anyway!', at which point I retired triumphant into obscurity. In the coffee shop someone said to me, 'You went on so long I thought you were in charge of the event.' And towards the end of the afternoon I heard a well-known critic feeding Beuys a string of fawning questions agreeable to the expected answers; so my intervention had hardly perturbed the proceedings. It would perhaps be salutary to see what the film camera made of it.

'Outside the Gallery System' was the title of an article Peter Joseph and I published in *Studio International* in 1969, partly as manifesto, partly as prelude to the installation of two outdoor works in the grounds of the Iveagh Bequest at Kenwood on Hampstead Heath. Both of us were moving away from paintings on canvas at that time; we wanted to use wider dimensions that would implicate the viewer's or participant's own location and movement. The Heath, and Kenwood in particular with its fine art collection and its eighteenth-century parkland, was very familiar to us; we had walked and argued and agreed there countless times, but it was still a surprise and delight to us when we approached the curator, John Jacobs, that he so readily fell in with our plans and saw the proposal through his committee. Peter's contribution consisted of three flat discs about eight feet in diameter, of a pure bitter yellow, to be propped against trees, several hundred yards apart, in an open area of gentle slopes; they were, I wrote, 'signals that conveyed nothing except their own position'. Mine was called 'Four-Colour Theorem' after the famous and then still unsolved mathematical problem in topology; it was a collection of about a hundred pieces of hardboard, from eighteen inches to four feet across, of four different shapes and colours, laid out on a large lawn in a walled garden, to be rearranged at will by whomsoever chose to engage with them. The exhibition attracted a good deal of notice and, as we had hoped, the people who interacted with these creations were largely non-gallery-going, dog-walking, hand-holding, icecream-eating happeners-by. However, interaction steadily escalated into destruction. Young anarchs discovered that my pieces could not only be set side by side in the two sober dimensions I had allotted them but upended and driven point-first into the lawn, or sent sailing through the air. After a Bank Holiday weekend we found that one of Peter's discs had vanished from the glades and my theorem had been sacked by skinheads and thoroughly disproven.

Later that year, retreating to the safety of 'the gallery system', Peter and I contributed two large projects to a four-person show called 'New Space' at the Camden Art Centre. Peter's was a seventy-foot-long head-high wall of yellow-painted canvas almost bisecting the room it was built in, a severe stretching of the viewer's kinaesthetic reactions, which achieved the honour of being denounced by George Steiner for its dumb hostility to language. Mine, 'Moonfield', was based on the same geometrical shapes as 'Four-Colour Theorem', but this time painted black on one side and white on the other. Initially they were laid black-side-up on a black floor in a blacked-out gallery space; as people found them and turned them over so that they became visible to dark-adjusted eyes, a shifting puzzle-landscape came into existence. This show constituted both zenith and moonset of my brief arc across the skies of modern art.

A number of large art-projects occupied my mind over the next year or two; some of these still seem to me worthy of realization, but none of them emerged into actuality. What I produced tended to the casual-looking – scatterings of wooden rods painted black and white – and even to the invisible – mere dots on my studio walls. Thus my work became an almost totally private and meditative activity, and eventually there was so little for anyone to see in it that the move from making visible objects to putting words into a notebook which could be shut at the end of each day was a small one, and my final disappearance to the Aran Islands hardly caused a ripple of talk in circles which perhaps once had had hopes of my career. The last work of those London years was a yard-long white rod that hung vertically in the middle of the studio, suspended by dozens of fine coloured threads. I called in Guy Brett to witness to its existence; then it was taken down thread by thread, and wrapped away for a long time. I left the visual for the verbal, we left London for Aran.

Twenty-five years later, long after we had moved from Aran to Connemara, I thought I would like to have another look at this work, so we put it up again, in a rather low and cluttered space, in which it nevertheless cast a spell. Coincidentally about that time a Michael Tarantino phoned, introduced himself as a freelance art curator, and invited me to participate in an international exhibition he was arranging at the Irish Museum of Modern Art, to be called 'The Event Horizon' in reference to an essay by

Antonioni. No doubt he had in mind my maps, which he knew of, and perhaps he was rather alarmed when I told him that I had in fact worked in the visual arts long ago and would like to show a piece from that era; but he could hardly withdraw at that stage. So M and I restrung the rod with longer threads, wrapped it up again and carried it to Dublin. IMMA's spacious halls and chambers in the grand neoclassical building of Kilmainham rang with activity; complex and cryptic installations were being mounted: a huge photographic panorama of fashionable young people behaving strangely by London's Sam Taylor-Wood, an array of twelve video monitors showing a flock of sheep by Canada's Atom Egoyan. We were shown our allotted room; it was large, lofty, bathed in light from a tall window. Deferential assistants stood by with a great scaffolding platform on wheels, ready to help us create something of international significance. We undid our small bundle. The threads had worked themselves into a dreadful tangle. A needle was sent for, and M picked away at the knot for an hour. Then we gave up, apologized to everyone, retired to a friend's house, and spent the next day unravelling the mess. Returning to the gallery, we found that the rest of our exhibit had been unpacked and hung. The originals of my three maps occupied a side room, and round the walls of the main room were the panels of text I intended should throw some light on the meaning of the installation. This time the hanging rod unfolded its wings and embraced the splendid space with ease and grace. I'm not sure that many people grappled with the post-modern wrap-around of interpretations I'd given this item of high modernism; but who cares? The thing-in-itself was beautiful.

Left Hand

One summer's evening in my twentieth year as I lay half asleep in a field near Avebury, I watched a painting brushed into being on the black of my interior ground. A honeyed glow, increasing in brightness as it advanced to the left, identified itself as the play of light across the woodwork of an old, varnished, kitchen dresser. The golden brown modulated to a silvery white and then darkened slightly around the outline of a head. This was a 'Last Supper', or (I now think) a 'Supper at Emmaus', and the painter was Rembrandt. With full, firm, strokes he put down black with thick streaks of white in it for the hair. Next, the ear: one stroke of the palest ivory composed the rim and lobe, and the rich, dark, convolutions within were created with smooth, exact, touches. And all the while he kept up a quiet sing-song chant: 'This will never do at all! This will never do at all!'

Intense though it was, this epiphany soon faded from my mind, and only the chance discovery of a letter written immediately after the event, which came back into my possession some thirty years later, enables me to re-experience it now. What does it furnish me with, apart from a possible rueful epigraph for a more personal tally of my work as a painter? (It is because all my dealings with the art-world's institutions recounted above seem so flippant and unengaged – my right hand, my shaking-hands hand, knowing not what my left, my painting hand, was so serious about – that I undertake a second telling.) At least this ghostly masterclass reminds me of the sensuous delight of the act of painting, for instance of using an almost liquid mix of oil or acrylic paints to produce an even colour-field, the smooth flow of paint flooding the bays and rounding the horns of a drawn outline, the creamy verge spooling off the corner of a flat brush to form a thread-thin tideline mating millimetre by millimetre with that laid down from the other side of the boundary. Doing this swiftly across a large area delineated by a precise arc right across the canvas, never letting any part of the advancing margin stagnate and go flat for more than a few seconds before catching it up into freshness, was a skill I acquired with great pain over some years and deployed with success only in a few big geometrical abstract works of the late '60s. At an earlier period I had revelled in a calligraphic immediacy, the thrill of the win-all lose-all gesture, the molten moment of an action perhaps deeply premeditated but physically unrehearsed. Those were ink-drawings of ecstatic nature-spirits, half tree half bird, dashed off with a broad brush that could feather across the surface leaving a haze fading to nothing, or turn on its edge to inscribe a narrow ribbon, or twist to screw a black vortex into the paper.

But these times of joy in capability were separated by protracted, sullen, unsuccessful, struggles, particularly with my recalcitrant colour-sense. Why for so long I did not take proper notice of the fact, known to me since my teens, that my red-green colour-discrimination is defective, I do not understand. Perhaps it was that the term 'colour blindness' seemed to be such a misnomer. My world is as brightly, subtly and variously coloured as anyone else's; reds in particular could not be redder, could not be more different from green. But sometimes from other people's behaviour I learn that reds call out to them from the margins of vision in a way they do not to me. For instance once I entered a woodland glade and was walking across it when my companion, a few steps behind me, cried out in surprise at a circle of big orange-red toadstools close by. As soon as I looked at them, they were as intensely and indeed alarmingly coloured as could be – but they had not caught the corner of my eye. Also, pale or greyish pinks and mauves can be ambiguous; in fact I feel them as treacherous, ready to change their affiliations from red to blue behind my back. So, looking back on them now, I have to admit that a number of my paintings suffer from this disability. I can see that they are wrong but cannot see how to mend them. The exceptions are works in black and white, or in earth tones, or in colour-pairs that serve only to differentiate one form from another. The works that 'will never do at all' are to be culled as I drag them out for this retrospective of my painting career; the rest may subsist in cupboards and attics for the indefinite future.

Why have so many of them followed me around to this date? I have to face my reluctance to destroy even the most embarrassing juvenilia. It is not that they lead me back like a trail of footprints to valuable and otherwise unrecuperable states of being. Is this a self-portrait? A boyish head, the mask of the face removed as if bulldozed from within, leaving a rim of cracked masonry around the hole, in which appears an uninhabited, dislocated, cityscape of tilted pavements and windowless façades under the light of a streetlamp. The background to the head is a brick wall topped by spikes, over which dangle two dead-looking hands on wrists like knotted sheets. There are several other drawings from my teens that hardly emerge from psychic symptomology into art. One oil I will keep, as I remember feeling it was my first proper painting: a realistic, face-on, view of a drab little urban park seen through its iron railings, with a pavement and gutter in the foreground, lopped trees behind the railings, and in the background some terraced houses under a slate-grey winter sky. Since the circumstances of my early years were free, enabling and supportive, it seems almost unjust to perpetuate these images. I can account for them – for the imprisoned selves who peer through the bars of these dreary scenes – only in terms of teenage anxieties social and sexual, which are not of much interest, being the common lot outside of Margaret Mead's fabled Samoa. They contrast with other early works in which a generalized figure, a protagonist, is caught up by the rhythm of forms into a swirling, pantheistic, world of birdsong or cathedral arches, or stands reverentially gazing from an architectural ope onto multiple views of moons breaking through clouds or setting on sea horizons. These almost allegorical scenes suffer on an old dilemma that has embarrassed better artists than me, of whether Mankind, the Child, the Soul, should be nude, or draped in timelessly indeterminate robes.

Perhaps in these evidences of painful conflict between my longing for sensuous and intelligent breadth to life, and the frustrations of shy and inhibited adolescence in a torpid country town, I can see, if not the very origin, then the first apparition of a dualism that has riven almost all my creativity. In the abstract paintings I misspent so much effort on in Cambridge – most of them unexhibitable even to myself and long since destroyed, the rest shortly to follow them – there is an interplay between a gridwork of horizontal and vertical divisions that seems to derive from the earlier bars and railings, though it is more supportive than oppressive, and freeform motifs that vary from the ecstatic intertwining and soaring of flame or bird-flight, through a Beardsleyesque swordplay elegance, to the stressful jaggedness of Herbert Read's 'geometry of fear'. A dialectic of reason and emotion animates all art, and it would be simplistic to locate it in the opposition between the rectilinear and the irregular; there is nothing rational about the right-angle *per se*, and while Mondrian's supremely instinctual balances breathe rationality, paintings constructed according to algorithms often smell of laborious dottiness. However, two principles of organization are at work in these Cambridge paintings: a flow of energy, muscular or nervous, and a stasis, of stability or rigidity. I shall keep just one of them; its vortices of interlacing espaliered on Cartesian co-ordinates look forward to my much more recent concern with the contrasted geometries of the Celtic and classical worlds.

It was not remarkable that in Vienna, having for the first time organized my life to privilege the hours of painting, I should at first find myself unable to paint. Eventually I broke out of a period of paralysis by, almost arbitrarily, sketching some free versions of an engraving by Vesalius – one of his shocking visions of the human frame stripped of clothes and skin. From these grim anatomies sprang a race of monsters, gaunt gesticulating lop-limbed spider-dinosaurs with empty skulls. Unleashed upon the city of Freud, the exorbitantly phallic and castrated things (sprouting phalluses as the Hydra sprouted heads) fell upon their inevitable interpretations as upon swords; nevertheless I think they had non-personal connotations, in that time of impending warfare between 'Neanderthals with atomic weapons', as a Viennese friend of ours put it, and at that place where human creatures had bayonetted and flung grenades at each other on our very doorstep little more than a decade earlier. Horrible as they are, some of these figures could be worth preserving. They were rapidly sketched on big sheets of cartridge paper, in triangular brush-strokes of black ink that give them a texture of bark; in fact if they seem about to fall on one like trees, they are not ancient, gnarled and blasted oaks but light, wind-thinned upland birches or bare wintry rowans. Behind their menace they are fragile creatures that remind me as I write of a praying mantis that came once to pose, rigid as a spun-glass ornament, in the lamplight on my pillow in Turkey. In these characteristics they showed some saving affinity with the lyrical sequence of both tree-like and bird-like feminine figures, Winged Victories in fact, which were painted at about the same time.

My murderous male hominids soon acquired habitats to prowl in: claustrophobic tunnels and cellars and slits that might have been between hammer and anvil or the jaws of a screw-vise. Later the pathetic creatures skulked in the crevices and drains of cities of unworldly purity, whose streets were glittering perspectives between towers that threatened infinity and converged on cold stellar discs. Looking back on them I can see that these intolerably perfect 'Cities in a Vacuum' would have been more effective expressions of a derelict human condition without their grotesque and miserable inhabitants. In fact an artist of our acquaintance among the Viennese surrealists told me as much, but I could not accept it at the time. And perhaps there are no shortcuts; one should not counterfeit unity by suppressing conflictual elements. Mercifully, both figures and settings gradually abstractified themselves, turning into energetic coiled forms trapped within or springing free from geometrical constraints.

Soon after our move to London a way forward opened into a coherent evolution that was to continue for six or seven years. The new paintings were calm and contemplative in tone, abstract but suggestive of astronomical transits and occultations. (I love eclipses. Just as the flow of clouds past sky-places marked by treetops can suddenly arrest one's attention and indue a self-realization as a localized earth-surface entity, so the grand slow closing and opening of the lunar or solar disc can cast the mind out like a shadow wheeling across the spaces of our sidereal voyage.) The first series of paintings of this new dispensation were entitled 'The Dreams of Euclid', and their subtext or sub-imagery concerned the psychology of creativity; these were forms intuited just before they cohered into theorems, mysteries about to be resolved by reason, or (since they could be read as processes glimpsed in their ongoing in either direction) certainties being perturbed, diagrams nodding off into reverie. Some of them were as much as five or six feet square, and a typical example contained one large shape bounded by two compass-drawn arcs with centres separated horizontally by an inch or less, giving an outline just perceptibly broader than a perfect circle. (In the Venn-diagram sense, the shape would be the union of two circles.) The centres themselves were marked by pairs of tiny circles, or paired constellations of circles, of radii equal to their separation, giving a measure of the stress and potential fission of the whole. Later canvases were more complex, with a square array of sixteen or twenty-five circles, touching or overlapping, on which a slightly tilted or distorted grid of the same number of rather smaller circles would be superimposed, the second set being the same hue as the background, so that the crescents and annules left visible of the first set appeared like phases of an eclipse in a contradictory, depthless space.

In the late summer of 1968 I took myself off to France, not to the streets of Paris where the imagination was still violently asserting its right to power, but to the quiet roads of the Vaucluse and the Camargue, where I walked and hitchhiked, alternately baked and drenched, for a few weeks, and came back with the germs of a new series of paintings. These were square canvases hung from a corner so that one of the diagonals was horizontal. The simplicity of the shapes within them, bounded by circular arcs and straight lines, seemed dictated by the same urgency of communication as those of road signs. They were shown in an exhibition at the Lisson later that year, for which occasion I wrote this note:

The boundaries of a rectangular canvas can usually be taken as purely conventional indications of the limits of the artist's interest in the space he is depicting or creating: on the picture surface a statement is made to which the edges add the phrase 'and so on', or 'nothing of interest beyond here'. By hanging the canvas diamond-wise one transforms the situation; the corners demand attention, the edges assert their reality, and the surprising length of the diagonal is displayed. The canvas acquires a powerful though ambiguous directionality; its vectorial energies are conducted by the corners into the surrounding space, which is really, and not merely conventionally, distinct from the space of the painting. By asserting its limits and orientation the canvas attains its stature as an object in space.

Beyond that, the present paintings are transcriptions of my own experiences 'as an object in space' – specifically, of the freedoms of a solitary walking-tour, of travelling towards the sun or following a map, the purely topographical sensations of seeing a range of hills, approaching it and crossing it.

A range of paradoxes appears on the horizon; poetic answers to logical questions, the rational solution of problems the posing of which is an irrational act.

My preferred territory lies between aesthetics and logic.

Another factor that made these new paintings things in themselves rather than depictions of (abstract) shapes, is that the forms within them were partly outlined and defined by the edges of the canvas. Retrospectively, I see this as the shedding of the last traces of anthropomorphism (teratology, I should say, in view of the Viennese nightmares), for in the preceding paintings even the purely geometrical elements – circles and the sums or differences of overlapping circles – were shown as if arrested and observed in their interactions; they were protagonists. Paradoxically, this step towards the sculptural led to another, in its way a reversion to the painterly, which was to cut out the forms in board and let them find their bearings and interrelationships on a wider ground, the ground itself. This was the internal genesis of the 'environmental' artworks of a hundred or more flat pieces I created in the walled garden at Kenwood and in the Camden Arts Centre. In evolving the shapes of these pieces I played around with circular arcs of various radii drawn within a basic square until I found four that formed a geometrical family; because of their internal relationships an indefinite number of theorem-like arrangements can be found when the resultant shapes are laid down next to each other. I incorporated many of these configurations in a drawing which was later turned into a screen print for me by Kelpra Studio. For the real-life version, 'Four-Colour Theorem', shown at Kenwood, I scattered the pieces on a smooth lawn as an invitation to direct participation:

At first they lie at random, a field of colour into which the spectator walks, and then, as people begin to rearrange them and discover their interrelationships, areas of order spread, merge, clash and dissolve. The activity, the building of a landscape, rather than any end-product, is the art form.

That was the theory as I expressed it at the time in an article for *Studio International*, and to a degree it worked. Guy Brett wrote:

Timothy Drever's are unusual shapes arrived at by simple and logical geometrical decisions, and their colours are unusual too, not merely wholesome primaries. If you move them about on the grass you find that they do not lock together to form any final solution: their 'order' is something more tenuous and subliminal (and therefore probably more open to individual invention). I noticed that few people cared to arrange the whole number, and if you stepped back and treated the painting as a spectacle you could see various small areas of decision left by different people.

Later in that year came the long evening of the first moon-landing, seen on TV as a dreamlike series of unstable and almost incomprehensible black-and-white images. From these visual impressions a new version of the work was born, as I described in an article for the special 'moon' number of Miron Grindea's *Adam International Review*:

Lunar paradoxes: one flies towards a symbol of inconstancy, ambiguity and madness, to alight upon a surface of weatherless scientific candour; after the longest voyage one steps from the space-craft into an indoor environment, that of the hermetically sealed, soundproofed, sterilised laboratory; the first exploratory step alters what is to be explored more than a million years have done.

'Moonfield', an environmental work, is an indoor version of a work called 'Four-Colour Theorem' which was exhibited on a lawn in the grounds of Kenwood last May.... This work had a brief and eventful life; after weathering a week of storm and sunshine it was smashed by a bored bank-holiday gang. The roughly painted white undersides of the pieces were left showing here and there among the fragments. Later, brooding over the death of this work, I found that image of its destruction merging with the memory of the strange white night of the first moon-landing. Thus when the opportunity arose of making a large indoor work for the Camden Survey '69 show, a link had already been effected in my mind

between the lunar surface and the ghostly remembrance of the Kenwood project, between the Sea of Tranquillity and the protectiveness of an indoor environment. The work had to be rethought. In the open it had been colourful, extrovert, intimately reactive to every change in the sky; the new version would be stark, calm, mysterious, precise, withdrawn.

'Moonfield' uses the same four geometrical shapes as the earlier project, but now the pieces are black on one side and white on the other. The floor is black, and the lighting so subdued that when the pieces are black side uppermost they can only be found by touch; they can be lost and rediscovered – visually they are recreated by being discovered. Each person entering the dark gallery finds a new surface, at first unintelligible, which is the record of his predecessors' explorations and will be recreated or annihilated by his own investigations.

Lurking in the darkest corners of the gallery, hoping to discover what it was that I had made, I watched people at work with 'Moonfield'. Little children and civil servants pieced together flower-shapes of greater or lesser elaboration. A critic perched on the edge and sighed, 'If one had the energy....' A religious maniac constructed gigantic jewelled Byzantine crosses and immediately destroyed them. A group of art-students heaped the pieces layer upon layer in a glimmering confusion, a nebula which the next comer dispersed into geometrical constellations. Another group abolished the whole field by turning all the white sides down. At first I was critical of some of the effects produced, but that of course was to look upon the work as a 'participational' piece in which I abdicated the artist's right to choose to the spectators. Finally I would like to see it as a work the medium of which is people's actions, structured and rendered symbolic by the structure of what they handle. The 'states' of 'Moonfield' are not works of art, they are momentary records of people's visions, timidities, urges towards symmetry, towards chaos. The 'work' has its being in a structured flux of activity; it is the process of exploration.

Over the next year or two I conceived a number of large-scale installations, but none were exposed to the light of existence. One of them took the neglected aspect of 'Moonfield', the floor itself, and developed it into what I called a 'structured arena'. I quote from an article I wrote on the mathematics of it for a journal of 'computer arts' Gustav Metzger edited:

... This [experience of watching people interact with 'Moonfield'] led me on to think of ways of creating areas which would impose certain rhythms on anything taking place within them, and on the consciousness of anyone entering them. One project I considered was a concrete floor of regularly spaced shallow waves, perhaps 4 inches high and just over a stride from top to top; the area covered would be large enough for a specific rhythm to be generated by the act of walking across it. This floor would not be presented as a finished art-work but as an arena for experiment by myself or anyone else. It would be interesting to try different lighting effects, for example; a strong overhead lighting, with the floor painted white, would make the surface difficult to read as one walked over it; illumination by a flickering candle down in one corner would turn it into a sea of pulsating shadows. Again, people could explore it and discover its structure by touch, in complete darkness.

On this continuously curved surface one could experiment with discontinuous 'additions'; a scattering of rigid, fragile, 'measuring rods' would change its character; footballs would bounce on it quite unpredictably; various amounts of water would convert it into a series of ponds, and then into a series of islands. Musical, dance or theatrical groups could let the rhythms of their own activities interact with its periodic structure. In general the interest would lie in the 'interference' of the floor's stable and coherent wave-structure with the unstable and fluctuating forms of action superimposed upon it.

Another of these unrealized projects was the result of following the train of thought, or at least the mathematical doodling, behind my arcs and squares into the third dimension. Geometrically it concerned the largest circle that can be drawn within a cube, and constructionally it was to be realized as a ring of three- or four-inch steel tubing 30 feet in diameter, exhibited in the smallest cubic chamber that could hold it (which works out at just under 25 feet in each dimension). The ring was to be a deep Chinese-lacquer red and the chamber white. Entrance and exit doors were to be arranged so that the viewer had to step through the ring, and before entering, to enhance the element of ceremonial, one would have been given a simulacrum of the ring small enough to be carried in the palm of the hand. Would have been! ... I went so far as to contact a steelworks, whose engineer became quite interested in the problem and did some calculations on the thickness of tubing necessary for the ring not to sag, but I took it no further.

In truth, although I have traced the evolution of my London paintings and installations as if it took place in the serenity of that 'preferred territory between aesthetics and logic', there were emotional forces driving it. One of these was my progressive disgust with the commercial aspects of the art world. Whatever art was, I felt (in anti-structuralist mood), it had to be the opposite of money; hence the move from the plutocracy of the private galleries to open, public, spaces. However, the public arena too was contaminated by the blurring of boundaries between art and publicity, between artist and celebrity. Although 'Moonfield' had been well received I felt psychologically unable to set about persuading money-men of the worth of these further projects, and they came to nothing. But in any case I was in retreat from such episodes of public exposure into the silence – sometimes a contemplative happiness, sometimes a distraught paralysis – of my studio, and my ethical queasiness was, if not a rationalization – nothing could have been less rational – then a symptom of a deeper unease. For ever since the year of 1968 a wind had been blowing through my mind; it had blown me around Provence in that year, then to Norway to pay my respects to the midnight sun, and soon it was to blow me to the Aran Islands. No doubt the same wind had acted on such artists as Richard Long and Hamish Fulton, and many others who quitted the city for the wilderness at that time. In a recent essay I described that period, and the less than minimal art produced in it, as follows:

During the two years in which I was shrinking myself out of the London artworld, the works I produced became increasingly smaller and more private, dwindling finally to dots that even friends visiting my studio rarely noticed. Some of these 'points' as I called them were little round objects such as washers dropped in the gutter by people servicing their cars on Saturday afternoons, which I noticed, although not consciously looking for them, during the long abstracted country walks I used to take at that time, orienting myself by glimpses of the spires of Kilburn, Cricklewood and Neasden, or by the rumble of trains whose radial escape-routes seem to have determined the layout of the nevertheless hopelessly dull infill of late nineteenth-century housing between the crooked hearts of those onetime villages. I used to try to recover what exactly had been running through my head at the instant my eye was caught by one of these bright pavement-flowers, and sometimes back at home I would put the little disc on my index fingertip, add a drop of glue, and affix it to a wall by the act of pointing to the spot it was to occupy, so that it became what some analytic philosopher I was reading at the time calls a 'point of ostention', the point at which a line drawn from and in the direction indicated by a pointing finger first intersects a solid surface. Or I would post one off to a friend with instructions to throw it away somewhere in the house, to forget it, to find it by chance after many years, and to let me know what exactly had been the mental content of that moment of rediscovery. Although I have never received any such reflected gleams from distant consciousnesses, at home I did occasionally notice a visitor's gaze, idly straying across blank surfaces, suddenly arrested as a reflex of sight focused attention on one of the dots I had set like traps around our rooms; then I would know that a moment had been picked up, salvaged from the blind onrush of time, that an unknown significance had arisen, like the curl of a questionmark from a full stop, out of an event almost as bare and minimal as one of relativity theory's space-time data.

Just before I achieved invisibility I created the three works that were to be seen publicly only after a lapse of quarter of a century, in 'The Event Horizon' at the Irish Museum of Modern Art in Dublin. The first of these was a collection of wooden rods of lengths from about three to eight feet and of thicknesses from an eighth of an inch to eighteen inches or so, painted in black and white bands in various combinations of width. They used to lie stacked in a loose bundle in a corner or all crisscrossed on the floor in a way that reminded me of my grandmother's little set of ivory spillikins. In a letter to my parents I wrote:

Quite how they form a work of art I don't know. If I arrange them, or hang them on the wall, or tie them together into structures, I invariably diminish them. So it seems the relationships that unite them are not their spatial interrelationships. Rather, they form a family, or as Peter says, a single growth. He is coming across the same problem in his latest paint-

ing, which shows three block-shapes side by side on the canvas. But it doesn't work as a painting. It's curious that his coloured sketch for it works very well, perhaps because it's on a page with another scribble or doodle, and so one accepts the page itself as a mere support for the paint. But put the same form on a canvas and one becomes conscious of the space around and between the blocks, which then look 'artistically' placed within the borders of the canvas. Result, the blocks seem to line up and face the spectator, instead of (metaphorically) facing each other. Same with my sticks. Even if I arrange them casually, the space they cover then has 'casual' written all over it. How does one arrange things in order to indicate that their arrangement is unimportant? In doing the sticks I was vaguely thinking about birdsong, the way different rhythms (from different birds) pass through each other, crisscrossing the garden. The geometry of their crossing is uninteresting – but the crossing itself, there's something I'd like to get at about that.

I produced one or two of these sticks each day until there were about thirty. The same sort of visual tick-tock ran through them all, but each had its own rate and rhythm, weight and balance, and I used to hand them one by one to whomever called to see them. An art-critical friend wondered if they were 'measure become organic', and indeed one might imagine them to be growth-stages in the life of a measuring-rod; perhaps I had unknowingly followed up the thought of measuring-rods that had arisen in connection with the wave-floor project. There used to be two or three very big sticks too, twenty or thirty feet long and several inches thick, which I suppose rightly formed part of the assemblage but were left outside leaning up into trees and have not accompanied me down to the present.

As to the second of these works, I have no memory of making it and was surprised after all those years when I found it wrapped up with the others. It consists of thirty-five thin white wooden rods each thirty-five inches long. On each one a different inch-long segment is picked out in grey, so that if they are laid side by side in a certain order the grey inch appears to progress regularly from one end to the other, but of course this symmetry is broken when they are dropped and scattered. Nowadays it is impossible for me not to read both these collections of rods as breakings-out from restrictive spaces – of the canvas, of the studio, of the art world, of the city.

The third piece was the slender, yard-long, vertically-suspended, white rod, which I used to think of it as measuring a pace taken towards the middle of the earth. It hung from dozens of coloured threads which converged to the centre of its upper end from drawing-pins set here and there in the ceiling and higher parts of the walls and furnishings of whatever space it was mounted in. When it inhabited the middle air of my studio it was mysterious and almost hypnotic in its stillness; I remember a visitor who slept on the floor under it one night saying how much she had learned from it. The simplicity of the white rod seemed to disengage itself from the prismatic mist of threads like a decision from a multitude of indefinite considerations. Retrospectively I know it was obscurely at work in our decision to leave London for the Aran Islands.

None of these three works had names so far as I can remember, but now I call them, respectively, 'Autobiography', 'Inchworm', and 'To the Centre'. When I resurrected them in 1997 I was disturbed to realize that in their abstraction they prefigured a whole network of imagery – of gravity and rainbows, of compass roses and cardinal directions, of the birth of the universe and the moment of vision – I had thought originated in the intervening period of map-making and topographical writing, my geophanic years. In the 'Event Horizon' show at IMMA I confronted the latent intentions of these three constructions with passages from the subsequent writings, exhibited on wall-mounted cards. The title of the installation as a whole, 'The View from the Horizon', hinted at my unease as to whether any of this work would do at all. The move from city to island, from the visual arts to literature, from minimalist abstraction to the most scrupulous cartography of the grain of the actual – had even that drastic step not been enough to shake up my little store of conceptions? Have I only painted the one problematic onto my interior darkness during all the career reviewed here? To the artist it is intolerable that one cannot climb to one's own horizon and look beyond.

THICKETS AND DARK WOODS

I suspect that all my memories of the house in Braiche Close, Redbourne, which we left when I was four, are reconstructions from old snapshots, except for an image of crisscrossed diagonals, the leading of its diamond-pane windows, which feels as if it has been impressed permanently on my vision by the intensity of my staring through it. My parents used to recall that I would stand with my nose against one of these windows looking out at evening shadows gathering in the garden; 'There's a tiny dark,' I would say, and 'There's another tiny dark.' Darkness reveals space; would I have noticed these little tents of space under bedding plants or tufts of grass if the sun had not declined to illuminate them?

My father was able to see into the depths of leafage that presented opaque surfaces to most eyes; therefore he was able to show us children the scribble on a yellowhammer's egg even if he could not decipher it. On caravanning holidays after the war he used to conduct us on tiptoe walks along sun-warmed field margins, where it seemed nothing in the hedgerow bottoms escaped him; he could dip the handle of his walkingstick into the mesh of twigs and hook out a shiny green grass-snake for us to fall upon and try to grab as it writhed in figures of eight and disappeared as cleverly as if it had swallowed itself. Padding softly along the byways of the leafy heartlands of England in the pantheistic hush of twilight, I learned wordlessly from him to look. I brought glow-worms back to the caravan in a jamjar, and stared at them, or into them, for hours after bedtime, fixated by the living light emanating not from their surface but from their cloudy interiors, and then, a night or two later, experienced the joy of discovering that they had laid eggs, each with its own minute yolk of luminescence.

I inhabit darkness confidently, moving cautiously, absorbing wide-eyed the vaguest of glimmers and pallors, actively interpreting them as presences and emptinesses. Once, coming home from school on a full-moon night when the ground was covered in snow, I challenged my opponent in snowballing to a duel in a neglected little woodland park. As soon as we were among the spindly trees I stood as still as one of them, and let him go on before. Soon he had no idea where I might be, whereas I could trace him clearly by the suddenly jutting angles his nervous movements produced in the motionless columnar silhouettes of the treetrunks between us. I waited until he was quite bewildered by perspectiveless black and white, and cautiously lobbed a snowball over his head into the stiff rattling leaves of a laurel bush; he leaped around in a panic, and I had to call out to calm him. A few years later, in Malaya, I found myself on the other side of the shadows, when the rota of guard duties had me prowling a bomb-dump from two till four one night. The bombs lay, profoundly asleep, in long lines between high embankments that divided a few acres of rough ground into pools of blackness. Palmtrees rose out of the undergrowth, their fronds creaking high overhead.

Beyond the barbed wire, swamp and jungle croaked and groaned and shrieked. There was a frisson of danger, slight enough to be enjoyable, for although we had been told that the 'terrorists' had been driven from that locality they still haunted the night like the ghosts and goblins of only recently abandoned folk-belief. I wandered with my loaded rifle through this cemetery of moon-shocked iron, daring myself to penetrate its remotest alleys, and had my moment of panic when a firefly drifted in at head-height from the perimeter fence like the glow of an intruder's cigarette.

For many years after my National Service I lived in cities – Cambridge, Istanbul, Vienna, London – and could have denied my love of tangled obscurities had not briar-patches of doodling invaded the margins of every page I wrote, and had not many of my paintings been tussles with darkness ramified. Then I became a cartographer of the half-deserted and overgrown landscapes of the western seaboard of Ireland. The Burren, in particular, was to re-entrap me with the lure of thickets.

⋆

On a gloomy day, which was to prove the lowest point of some months of work in the Burren, I arrived at the ruined church of Kilmoon. I had heard that there was, or used to be, a stone carving of the head of a bishop in it, which had been employed for casting spells. Cursing-stones used to be known from many old religious sites in Ireland, and there is much folklore about the misfortunes – a sudden wind upsetting a boat, a neighbour's face struck crooked – caused by malicious persons turning such stones 'against the sun', that is, anticlockwise, while saying certain prayers. As late as the end of the nineteenth century a man, prosecuted for laming an old woman who had threatened to 'turn the stones of Kilmoon agin him', had pleaded self-defence and was acquitted. I found the little building roofless and full of nettles; I could not see the carved head, and a local man who came into the graveyard to help me search said that he hadn't set eyes on it for some years. So I noted the other features of the church and continued my mapwork up the road.

Later that day I happened to meet an elderly countryman who told me he looked after the church and could show me the bishop's head. It was beginning to rain heavily but he was not to be put off, so I walked back down with him, rather reluctantly. He went into a cottage for a coat, and we both climbed the stile into the long grass of the churchyard. He thoroughly believed in the power of the head; a priest once came out from the nearby village of Lisdoonvarna to put a stop to the pagan practice, he told me, but 'he hammered and hammered it and he couldn't mark it – and after, he didn't live a week!' It was difficult to follow his account, but I gathered that the bishop had got into trouble – 'too fond of the women' – and had been excommunicated; the phrase 'and Rome divides!' came into the story several times. When the Board of Works had tidied up the church the head had been thrown out with rubbish into the road, and this man's father had told him to put it back and look after it. I asked him if I should mention on my map that anyone who wanted to see it should apply to him? The idea alarmed him. If the Parish Priest (that old tyrant from the mountains) ever heard that he was showing the head to people, he'd get hammered as much as the old bishop was hammered, he said.

The door of the church was half walled up with blocks of stone, and he squeezed through under the little arch with great difficulty while I stood outside in the wet grass. He fished the stone out from nettles in a corner and humped it over and whacked it down in front of me on the wall across the doorway in a way that made me jump. He clearly believed that it was indestructible, contrary to the evidence of his own eyes that the face was featureless on one side. I felt a reluctance to touch the thing, but because he seemed to expect it, I 'took its likeness' (as he put it), sketching rapidly in the rain while he stood inside the church propping up the stone for me and saying encouragingly 'A fine hand! A fine hand!' It was a weird session, and helped to precipitate a mood of disgust with the sheer unreason of the Burren. Why, I wondered, was I standing in the rain listening to this garbled superstitious nonsense, when I could be at home listening to Monteverdi, or in Venice studying the architecture of San Marco, when the whole world of high culture was waiting for me?

In fact this wet stony landscape I was struggling with, day after day, week after week, was beginning to get the better of me. Some days were simply dispiritingly cold, solitary, wasted 'standing under a dripping bush halfway up Cowshit Lane' as my diary puts it, or in failing to find the Neolithic tomb I was groping through the thickets for, because the map-references given in the magisterial *Survey of Megalithic Tombs of Ireland* were incorrect, as I discovered in several cases. As it happened, I had other reasons for unhappiness at that time, but my isolation in the self-imposed task left me vulnerable; my diary records 'a crisis of loneliness' one evening in a rather chillingly proper guesthouse, after which I jumped onto my bike and pedalled furiously, almost blindly, for miles, met a woman who showed me a stone in the roadside wall with six fingerholes poked into it by a saint, one cannot imagine why, and then cycled back again from the site of the futile miracle – 'despair, almost, and an unsuccessful and exhausting fugue'. How, in the middle of my life, had I got into this dark wood?

★

Of course it was natural that having mapped the three Aran Islands I should raise my eyes to the mainlands visible from them: the purple shadowy peaks of Connemara to the north, the silver-mounded Burren to the east. In Robert Lloyd Praeger's book *The Botanist in Ireland* I found this bald mention, illustrated with a fuzzy photo of acres of *Potentilla fruticosa* scrub:

> Ballyvaughan is a small village on Galway Bay, with sufficient hotel accommodation, excellently situated for the exploration of Burren. A grassy valley runs S into the heart of the hills, with the grey terraced limestones rising on either hand …

It was enough to decide me. As soon as I had distributed the newly printed Aran map to the shops I took the plane to Galway, hitchhiked round Galway Bay to Ballyvaughan, had a Guinness in what was then the charming old-fashioned grocery-cum-bar opposite the quay, and walked back a mile to Lough Rask, where Dorie and Bernie's B&B looks down slanting fields to the trees of a heronry by a little lake. The weather was superb, sunny and breezy. I soon found myself at grips with, or in the grip of, this landscape's tight interlock of barrenness and exuberant fertility. My diary allows me to reconstruct my rambles and fervent amateur botanizing in some detail:

Ascension Day. Bernie and Dorie going to Mass at New Quay dropped me off at the corner for Corcomroe Abbey. I talked to the landlord in the pub there, who gave me directions and bought a map of Aran, and I strolled off feeling the pedlar's life is the best in the world. At the abbey, calves looking out of the windows of an ancient ruin covered in ivy, jackdaws and rooks perched about the abbey walls. I saw the tomb of the O'Loghlen kings of the Burren, whose descendants keep the pubs in Ballyvaughan. I crossed meadows from there to the main road and walked a few miles till I saw the famous turloughs[1] *down on the right. The biggest is a shallow oval bowl with a muddy pond at the bottom and shelving close-grazed meadow around marked in contours by whitish deposits. Around that again a ring of separate big boulders and thorntrees, and the blackish moss, no doubt Cinclodontus fontaniloides.*[2] *Cattle coming down one by one to drink. I spent a long time searching for Viola stagnina etc. Most of the ground was covered with dry strands of the pondweed Elodia canadiensis. I found the viola – small, bluish-white, long-leafed etc., but not decisively different from V. canina growing 10 or 15 ft. higher up. V. riviniana further up again among the bushes. Also saw amphibious bistort lying high and dry but very fresh (not in fl.). Plenty of silverweed, tormentil, creeping willow. Moving west I explored the margins of the woods: guelder rose, spindle tree etc. in flower, and came through shady tunnels to a marsh where pink 3-petalled Lesser Water Plantain was growing.... Then I set off over the hills to Ballyvaughan, but the hazel scrub led me directly up the slope instead of obliquely to the pass. I struggled through interminable belts of brambly woods thinking I'd soon climb out of it, but it went on and on, alternating with bare rocky patches and shady mossy coppices full of violets and sanicle. I came out at last and thought that something must reward me for the effort. And soon I heard a snuffle as a*

1. Turloughs are the transient lakes of Ireland's western limestone regions, that fill and empty through fissures in their basins as the groundwater level fluctuates.
2. A name as musical as falling water, which had stuck in my head from a study of the flora of turloughs by Praeger.

badger looked over its shoulder at me and went off. I sat down and waited, and soon its stripy face appeared in the bush. I walked round the bush and followed it as it worked along the bottom of a two-foot cliff, digging here and there and swallowing worms, I suppose, with noisy suckings. It took no notice of me; it was like taking a fat poodle for a walk. Eventually I stood within a yard of it, and when it took its head out of the grass it saw me and backed off with a snort. But it soon continued rooting and waddling on with me close behind. I must have spent half an hour with it.

Then straight up the mountain, and near the top in a little damp glen, dozens of fine yellow Welsh Poppies. I felt deeply rewarded. Coming down towards Lough Rask I saw a big hare go off and then stand just over a rise with its ears sticking up and its eye on me.

All the elements of the perfect West-of-Ireland day are in that – the old ruins with rustic life harmonious around them; the fascinating wildflowers (Praeger was the first to write in detail about the way different species of plant grow in contoured zones around the turloughs, depending on what degree and frequency of immersion they thrive on); the getting lost and coming out in a place where nobody goes, and the encounter with an animal that had never met humankind before and therefore was perfectly confiding; the discovery of a plant unknown in the region (and I was very proud of it, because the Burren has been so energetically searched by generations of botanists but this handsome tall poppy had never been recorded there); the magnificent walk over a hilltop into the sight of the ocean …

But that was holiday. The next year I came back in March to begin mapping in earnest. My method was simple enough: I carried the dozen or so sheets of the Ordnance Survey map that cover the region at six inches to the mile (topographically very accurate, though out of date, having been last revised in 1913-18), and I walked or cycled everywhere marking in new houses, paths, archaeological sites and holy wells, noting placenames and whatever local lore I could pick up. I had done some research beforehand, reading through a detailed and captivatingly discursive series of papers the Clare antiquarian Thomas Westropp published in the 1890s and 1900s, in which he set out to describe some of the principal ancient monuments, and was drawn into, as I was to be drawn into, a crazy attempt at full coverage. Westropp describes 310 Celtic or Early Christian ringforts and cashels in this region of some 150 square miles; I located them all on the maps and gave them numbers, and over a period of a few months visited each one to see if it was still extant, and found a lot more in the process. Similarly for the 66 Late Stone Age tombs, which had been published in 1960 in the *Survey of the Megalithic Tombs of Ireland*. My motive in trying to re-find all these things for myself was not just a concern for scholarly accuracy, it was a way of driving myself into every corner of the terrain – and it brought me sometimes to Eden, and sometimes abandoned me in thorns.

As population and land-use has fallen away over the century and a half since the Famine, hazel scrub, fraught with brambles, has eaten little fields by the hundreds. This secondary woodland appears quite timeless, a denial that culture had ever opened up these areas to the sun. Many of the trees are suspended in death, their rotten branches held in place by a thick glove of moss until one reaches to them for support in a difficult place, and they drop off soundlessly. A delicate haze of Herb Robert's thin reddish stems and mauve stars floats over the blanket of moss that covers the litter of boulders underfoot and the low mounds of collapsed field walls. With much puzzling and casting about I could often match the vagaries of these mounds snaking through the shadows with the crackle-glaze of field boundaries on my old Ordnance Survey maps, and use them to orient myself. (In an essay on the Burren I wrote at that time, I inadvertently stated that 'it is easy – but sometimes rewarding – to get bewildered and go wrong by 360° in these viewless thickets'. But an error of 360° brings one back on course, if one only knew it.) I spent many days badgering through these dim coverts looking for stone cashels which to judge by Westropp's descriptions had stood in open country a century ago, and which I found literally with my hands and were full to the brim with scrub; I climbed their tumbled but still mighty walls and paraded precariously around them at treetop level. The hazel reaches its most intractable in some of the closed depressions of central Burren, where depths of limestone tunnelled like worm-wood by long-vanished rivers have eroded and collapsed and been carted away by the Ice Ages. Exploration of one of these evidently left me too tired to write up my diary each night:

Poulacarran was overwhelming. It took me three visits to explore it, and there are a couple of ringforts I couldn't reach though I must have been within feet of them. I spent literally hours in the scrub on these almost vertical-sided hillocks around the long waterway, which I splashed across. Stillness, moist air, flies, cattle in the broad turlough. The first visit I looked around the church and down the track to the few ruined forts near the old cottages, the caves in the N-facing cliffs, the Tobarnarigh (no sign of any cult there), then up the cliffs and to and fro across the creigs south of the depression. A terrible fight through the dense bramble and hazel E from there until I burst through onto the open land where the 2 dolmens and a cist stand close together. Then all along the western rim of the valley – a great breezy sunny day – from one fort to the next, and tried to get down the cliffs at the head of it. Eventually I found a steep cattle track, a tunnel through shady woods, down by the boundary wall, and spent a long time scrambling up and down trying to find the double fort 'on a rock-dome in Meggagh'[3] *singing 'Where would you like to be? On a rock-dome in Meggagh with me ...', but no luck. The woods here unimaginably mysterious, great parcels wrapped in moss lying heaped everywhere, rotten branches that drop off at a touch – & yet even here traces of economic activity – a branch balanced across a stone-filled gap. Then on further down the track till I reached a little pond where bullocks were chewing the cud, and burst out into the open fields & crossed under the eyes of the houses to the Carron-Caherconnell road. Surely it wasn't the same day I visited the two big cahers there & found that the footpath still exists back through the valley to the old church – retracing that with another plunge into the unknown after a little ring up in a wood to the north. A bit of rain as I reached the turlough again. And cycled back to Kilfenora! Yes it* was *that day. I came again and spent another day around the Poulacarron itself & its rock domes, & then on another day coming over from Carron scrambled along the cliffs at the N of the valley and laid my hands at last on that elusive fort on the rock-dome in Meggagh. Why that one became such an object of ferret-like persistence I don't know. It's invisible from more than a yard away, and stuffed with impenetrable thicket. No, I've learned that there is no such thing as an impenetrable thicket. With time any length of any density of thicket can be traversed – lifting aside strand after strand of bramble, breaking apart forked trees, jumping here and crawling there. As I wrote to M, I'm great at acting out fables, & not so good at their morals.*

In this countryside clogged with the wreckage of its past, superstition presented itself with great immediacy. The stories I was

3. A phrase from Westropp's description.

told in so many cottages and fields had not yet sunk back into folklore; they were still news. This man, as a child, had taken all the coins out of a holy well reputed to cure warts, and the next day his hands were covered in warts. That family had built onto the west gable of their house, where the fairy paths are supposed to run, and had had no luck since. Even vision seemed warped by the force-fields of belief. A farmer showed me three low mounds (Bronze-Age barrows, in fact) on his land; 'They make a line!' he insisted, even though we were standing on one of them, another was straight ahead and the third off to the left. Similarly for three ruined castles a mile or two apart, north of the village of Noughaval; they 'made a line' which seemed to be of some unspecific significance for people of that neighbourhood, whereas on my map they made a rather irregular triangle. The *slua sídh*, the 'folk of the mounds', that is, of the ancient tumuli and ringforts regarded as fairy dwellings, are believed to travel in little whirlwinds, on the passing of which one should bow and take off one's hat, according to Westropp. As it happened my own encounter with them took place within distant sight of two of those dark ragged towers, out on the treeless levels of the townland of Cragnaruan. I say 'out' because it feels like a long, step-by-step journey from the world of roads and houses to reach this unfrequented and hazardous locality, the limestone being riven with fissures several feet deep, wide enough to break a leg in and hidden beneath a continuous carpet of moss. It was a hot afternoon, absolutely still except for an almost subliminal bourdon of insect life. I was picking my way across this expanse of mantraps, taking bearings of the castles just visible on the horizon since there were no other features higher than small hawthorn bushes and the decayed walls of abandoned fields to locate myself by, when I heard a car approaching. But surely I was a mile from any road? Within a few moments the sound had become that of swiftly flowing water – even more improbable in that desert of karst. Then suddenly the air around me was convulsed, it tugged at my cap and snatched at my map – and the invisible commotion was gone within a minute, rushing away into the distance, leaving all as before.

Sometimes I myself played the role of mischievous sprite. Creeping around in the hazel scrub one day, I found a number of stems recently cut for walking-sticks, and left them propped together in a little pyramid to puzzle whoever would come to collect them. Was I trying to immerse myself in this countryside to the point of vanishing? Some passages in my diary would almost suggest this; for instance my first visit to Oughtdarra in the southwest of the Burren. This is a valley of extremely complex topography ringed about with the ragged promontories and terraces of inland cliffs, every corner of which seemed to figure in scraps of folklore I'd read in Westropp. His succinct description of the place – 'One of the most complete labyrinths of valleys, cliffs, and enclosures, even in the tangled glens of the Corcomroes, lies behind the little ruined oratory of Oughtdarra' – and the observation of a person from that locality I'd met on my travels, that spring usually comes a week or two early to Oughtdarra, combined to instil an enchanting prevision of it into my overheating mind:

I had promised myself a sunny day in Oughtdarra – I don't know why this valley had taken on such significance – and I got it. A long swoop on the bicycle down from the hard-won height above it, bearing me irresistibly past one or two farms and around a narrow overgrown bend of a lane to the last little farm tucked away out of sight. I left the bike there and took a path around another hillock into the central and most secret hollow. Lots of tiny fields mainly overgrown, and the church itself so overgrown I wasn't at all sure I was looking at the right thing – other apparent gables shrouded with ivy at the eastern end of the hollow turned out to be just huge boulders. All around, densely thicketed crags, which I found encircled the hollow and separated it from a plateau at a slightly higher level. It took me some time to find my way up the crags and down onto this plateau and then up again to find the two little ringforts nearest the hollow. Then a sequence of decayed ringforts off to the north-west, and I discovered a good souterrain[4]*; and then the cliff peninsulas facing south towards the isolated conical fairy hill. Found the great wall of the peninsula fort. Then northwards to look for Leaba na hAon Bhó.*[5] *I found a boulder laying across two others to form a bed, and a vertical cleft in the cliff face behind it, and convinced myself that this was the cow's den and the cave in which would be found the Ulsterman who will give 'the last great stroke for Ireland'. I climbed up deep into the cleft and wrote with a stone on its wall 'Who is the man?' I was very excited by the culmination of my journey. (But I was in the wrong place, as I realized later.) I ate my chocolate there and an apple, and worked back to the kernel of the valley. I was too tired to face the bushes between the cliffs and the fairy hill.*

When I reached the first ring of crags I saw two men over on the other side of it crouching and stalking and watching a wild goat down among the fields. I came round to them, ducking through the bushes; they had a gun and were hoping to shoot the goat and its kids. I lay on the grass and we had a little talk, but they were intent on the goat and didn't know anything about the mythical cow etc. So I went down to the house and spoke to the woman there, who offered me tea as I had hoped. The cottage was full of animals – hens coming in for crumbs, cats coming and

4. An underground chamber, probably medieval.
5. 'The bed of the one cow', a site connected with a mythical and magically productive cow. Westropp gives the legend about the Ulsterman.

going, photos of tame fox cubs on the walls, and a most comic and pathetic sheepdog that sat under the table with big round eyes turned up in terror of the cat which it imagined was on the table and about to lean down and scratch it. Outside there was a pet lamb, and the woman told me that 'marten-cats' lived in the turf stack. She had heard that the 'one cow' had kept 20 families of poor people in milk who lived up there. She hadn't heard of the Ulsterman. I supposed that she had never been up the fairy hill, but she had, and at night too. And she told me a marvellously composed and consecutive tale about a dog which went missing. One night she woke up her husband and said she was going out to listen for it whining, because in the daytime she might not hear it with the buzzing of the bees and the birds singing. So she went all about the valley and up and down the cliffs listening and calling, and up the fairy hill and down it again, and at last she heard a little whine down in a cleft between two crags. She got her husband and he said, 'Well if it's down there you might as well forget about it.' But she found her way down into the gap with their other dog, and searched it from end to end without finding anything, until she noticed the other dog was looking up into a tree, and there it was stuck in the fork of a branch. It had fought with a fox up on the cliff and had fallen down into the tree. And she found the dead fox at the foot of the tree.

When I was leaving, the men were skinning a kid on the grassy hillock by the lane. I had another look at the church and found the carved holy-water stoup she had told me about, lying in the undergrowth. So many precious things lying like that in this countryside. A struggle up out of the valley again. I wonder if it is in danger from the bulldozing for land clearance that is going on SW of it. At the top I turned north and soon found a new track back down again that had to be explored. It divided up into three narrow boreens, and one became a vague path that delivered me back to one of the bush-covered rings I'd visited earlier. That was all very exhausting, and then a long ride back to Lisdoonvarna.

After a session of several weeks of such fieldwork I would cycle out of the Burren and round by Kinvara back to Galway – I remember the shock of my reflection in a shopwindow, as ragged as Robinson Crusoe – and, before taking the steamer back to Aran, spend a day in the library of University College, where the librarians, politely ignoring my feral aura, obligingly went gliding across the grey-carpeted expanses and up and down the stairs looking out historical, botanical, geological and geographical references to the Burren for me. On the last of these occasions I took out a library book that, from its title, promised well as antidote to all I had been through: Wittgenstein's *On Certainty*. At the time I made no personal application of Wittgenstein's remarks, my tendency always being to rush unreflectingly from one system of sensations to the next, from the physical to the intellectual, from thicket to theorem; but, looking into it again as I write, I am caught by this:

> If my friend were to imagine one day that he had been living for a long time past in such and such a place, etc. etc., I should not call this a mistake, but rather a mental disturbance, perhaps a transient one.

The context is a discussion of the status of certain statements claimed by other philosophers to be indubitable, to the denial of which no one could assent. Wittgenstein holds that if anyone did in all seriousness utter the denial of such a statement, we would not think him mistaken so much as deranged. That is, such statements are not really about the facts they seem to assert, but refer obliquely to the conceptual framework within which those facts are to be understood and justified. Had I really been living in the world my diary records, or was my Burren experience 'a mental disturbance, perhaps a transient one'? The facts asserted in the map I eventually deduced from that experience and published are implicitly tagged as geography, folklore, placename studies, etc. The whole layout of the map breathes order, lucidity, certainty. But through its precise gridwork show, I suspect, many tiny darks.

FIREWALKING

The 2500th anniversary of the Enlightenment of the Buddha fell during my year in Malaya, and I witnessed some extraordinary ceremonies. But it was a much humbler and more ambiguous ritual that made the deepest impression on me, at a local Tamil festival in honour of the Goddess of smallpox. The roomboy had tipped me off that there was to be firewalking, and this I was determined to see. I persuaded a fellow conscript to creep out of camp with me through the hole in the perimeter fence we used whenever it would have been self-defeating to explain the object of our egress to the guardroom at the gate. My comrade was a Plymouth Brother of massive faith and physique; the latter I had cause to appreciate that day, but I fear I despised the former attribute for its letter-by-letter literality. On our first encounter I had thoughtlessly mentioned that the biblical account of Solomon's great basin – 'ten cubits from brim to brim … and a line of thirty cubits did compass it round about' – implies that the ratio of the circumference of a circle to its diameter is three; as a technician who knew the value of π to several decimal places he had been upset by this and went to some pains in explaining away the anomaly. This slavish concern for fact was anathema to my florid High Anglicanism. Although by that period I no longer attended church, I still found it romantic to believe in the Real Presence of Christ in the sacramental bread and wine, because it was impossible; he, on the other hand took the sacraments to be purely symbolic.

I condense my letter home describing the event:

On the outskirts of the nearby village we met a procession dominated by a great chariot enshrining a figure of the malevolent Goddess, with pillars and crude statues and an elaborate dome supported by Devas (flying spirits), drawn by two white oxen in red and gold trappings, their horns in ornamented brass coverings. A large number of Hindus on a thick rope were helping to haul the chariot, with a lot of shouting and far too many people giving advice. Others were passing up offerings of food on little trays to three men perched on the chariot. Dozens of small boys were throwing coconuts onto the ground before the oxen to burst with a crash and splash milk everywhere. Among the crowd danced two men wearing tall wooden figures of a man and a woman with peepholes in their waists; the two giants bowed and rocked above the confusion of heads. Another man danced with a baton longer than himself, a strange slow dance with static posturings and smooth leaps; an old man battered a drum for him, and the group around him called on each other to try their skill. Behind the Goddess's chariot stepped slowly a singer and a group of men with little drums, odd wind instruments and cymbals, playing as fast as music can go, with a rattling rhythm and a swiftly rising and falling melody, vital, exciting, and finally crazing. There was also a band in uniform of some sort, with big drums and trumpets, playing a different tune. Each group of the straggling procession had its own heady music and moved at its own speed, stopping every few yards for more dancing; everyone was shouting, motorcars honked to get past, policemen moved slowly, ineffectually and resignedly. The men destined for the firewalking, garlanded in little white flowers, their bodies streaked with yellow, were in a group by themselves, quiet and detached. We hurried ahead to the field where the firewalking was to take place. A solid excited crowd was struggling around a small area isolated by a rough fence, with an arch at either end. Each of the tall palms sloping over the field had a line of boys all the way up its trunk. The crowd, mainly Tamil but with a lot of Chinese watching, was brilliant in saris and scarves of coloured silks. We pushed to get a view. I sat on my friend's shoulders – he is a vast fellow – and saw well. In the enclosure was a shallow pit about 18' long and 8' broad, heaped with smouldering charcoal. At one end was a trench full of water. We could feel the heat from where we were.

Thunder clouds were inking out the evening sky and the first heavy drops of rain hissed in the charcoal. The horizontal light of the setting sun caught the swaying tower of the chariot in greens, golds and reds as it lurched in the gateway and was dragged quickly across the field. The crowd swayed and shouted, the music gripped everyone in its rhythm as the climax approached. An excited face appeared in the narrow arch of the enclosure, a man forcing his way through the mob with his arms spread to hold back the firewalkers behind him. Four men with long rakes ran round the pit spreading out the coals, their faces twisted from the heat. Fruit and rice were flung into the pit. Then the first victim pushed through the archway; he looked tall and troubled. White powder was scattered over him, the crowd yelled, and he stepped onto the coals and strode out, staggered a little, took a few more long strides and jumped into the water. Another man was at the arch already, but he hung back, closing his eyes; they clustered round him shouting, slapping him, but he wouldn't go and they finally pushed him aside. The next I swear was a man I'd seen at the feast of

Thaipusam dancing exhausted under a tall contraption topped by the figure of a peacock, supported by a cage of sharp inpointing wires against his bare flesh. He walked out firmly with his head flung back, and halfway across he smiled like heaven's opening … And so they came one by one, some with tongue and cheeks pierced by skewers. Some had to be held back, some pushed on, some walked slowly with stately strides, some broke and ran halfway. But only that one so visibly possessed by God. As the last one jumped into the pit the crowd swayed forward with a roar, men hurled water onto the coals and a cloud of steam rose, everyone was shouting drunk with the rhythm of the hammering music. The boys slid down the palmtrees like drops of rain running down a wire. People scrambled to flick out bits of coal and gingerly wrap them in leaves to take home. And we went home too, having seen and felt too much for words.

Indeed I have had to omit words from the crux of this account, where I babbled of beatific love, atonement and other matters I knew nothing of.

The ardencies and exaltations of Hindu festivals, the vast quietudes of the Buddhist temples, were at least as convincing as the pale mystic rays I had once persuaded myself I saw emanating from the aumbry, when serving as altar-boy at an early-morning Mass that had drawn no worshippers but myself and the good Canon Wellington of St Margaret's, Ilkley. A dingy secondhand book I picked up in Penang (I still have it: B.K Sarkar, *Chinese Religion Through Indian Eyes*, Shanghai, 1916) also shook my unconsidered attachment to my parental faith, by its title as much as by its content: here was a survey of wide and ancient realms of belief, in which Christianity was only briefly considered, as 'the Christ-cult of Judaism', one of the numerous incarnation-myths of its time. By the time my stint in the RAF was done and I had reached Cambridge, my Christianity was a dead letter, and I had even abandoned an ingenious project of reconcocting God out of the immediacy of mystical experience, on the lines of Russell's construction of physical and mental realities out of sense data. Part of my induction as a freshman was an interview with the college chaplain. I took the opportunity of assailing this mild don with my observations on the weaknesses of the traditional proofs of the existence of God. He admitted he had only a hazy memory of them, but thought that even if each of them was faulty, collectively they were persuasive, to which I retorted that seven fallacies were no better than one fallacy. I remember his bowed head before me, with one lank lock forming a questionmark on its bare dome. But the exchange had convinced him that I was an advanced case, and, meaning well, he lent me a book on Christian spirituality. Ironically, its account of the nauseating self-mortifications of some medieval mystics finalized my departure from the fold.

*

I was not much concerned with either God or goddesses for many years thereafter, and my passionate unbelief was seldom discernible from the unthinking secularity of my various milieus, until in my late thirties I came to the west of Ireland, where the Angelus is still a rallying cry and the wayside grotto lurks to pick a fight with any passer-by. Even in the Aran Islands it was possible to manoeuvre my atheism down the twisty boreens of social practice without upsetting people too gravely. But when I got out into the field, as it were, my work – the mapping and writing-up of countrysides that are, or were, sacralized at various depths –

forced my attention on questions that still remain unresolved for me.

Our new postal address, for instance, brought the matter home: Kilronan, The Aran Islands. 'Kilronan' is from the Gaelic 'Cill Rónáin', the church or churchyard of Rónán (Gaelic *cill* being from a borrowing of the Latin *cella*, a cell). In undertaking my map of Aran, one of the tasks I set myself, blithely unaware of its difficulties, was to restore the musical and memorious Gaelic placenames that had been traduced by the phonologically dim and semantically null anglicized forms given on the official Ordnance Survey maps. This project I thought of as political, in that it aimed to undo some of the damage of colonialism and to uphold the local and vernacular against the levelling metropolitan culture of our times. But inevitably it was also a rescue-archaeology of a shallowly buried sacred landscape. Rónán was only one of the more obscure amongst the many hermits and monks who contributed to Aran's medieval fame as Ára na Naomh, Aran of the Saints. His holy well has long vanished, while his *cill*, from which the islands' chief village derives its name, is reduced to a knee-high rectangular enclosure a few yards square, featureless apart from a nineteenth-century cross-inscribed stone, and regarded (or disregarded, rather) as the saint's bed. Nothing is recorded of Rónán himself, but from the memories of one or two old folk of the village and the writings of a former parish priest I revived a story of how a Presbyterian bigot was smitten by a stroke when he tried to uproot an elderberry bush growing in the 'bed', which he said was a limb of St Rónán. The site is typical of hundreds I have sought out, formerly defended by popular reverence – indeed, superstitiously regarded as well able to defend themselves – and now neglected or forgotten.

Before Kilronan was developed as a fishing port in the late nineteenth century, Killeany, now a quiet and rather run-down village just over a mile to the south, was the centre of gravity of the islands. The name masks the foundation of St Éanna or Enda: Cill Éinne, and two assertions from the late medieval *Life of St Enda* will illustrate the interpretative situation facing the placelorist. First, that Enda was the brother-in-law of King Oengus Mac Nadfroích of Cashel in Munster, and received a grant of the islands from him in order to build a monastery. Secondly, that on reaching the mainland coast opposite Aran and finding no boat available, he and eight of his followers pushed a big stone into the water and sailed across on it. There is nothing implausible about the former proposition; Oengus is a well-attested historical figure (he died in 489 according to the *Annals of the Four Masters*), Aran was within the reach of his powers, and many Early Christian monasteries owe their inception to the patronage of a regional or local secular ruler. And as to the latter proposition, the very stone on which the saints came sailing in is still to be seen on the Killeany shore, close to the end of the airstrip. Now, one may accept the part of the story that sounds like history, or reject it as hopelessly unverifiable given that the earliest surviving written record of it dates from the fourteenth century, which is nearer to our own time than to Enda's – but the stone boat is headed for deeper harbours in the mind.

This canoe-shaped rock lying on the foreshore was not, for me, merely a picturesque relic of bygone, fanciful, naïve, folkloric times; in fact it became the cornerstone of an image of reality I was constructing through my maps and writings. St Enda's boat is the coming of history to Aran, symbolically its foundation stone. But this floating foundation stone itself is founded on nothing except the possibility of foundering like a stone. Just so, the cosmos has produced itself out of nothing and is maintained in existence by nothing, a perpetual, precarious wonder to itself, a miracle – perhaps the only miracle that ever happened, but that one all-inclusive. Although any given detail of it is in principle open to comprehension (that is, within the world there are no miracles), the whole overwhelms our intelligence by its richness; it is a plenum, a density of interrelationships, endlessly nourished by its own complexity.

In such a world every point is connected to every other point; every event is a starburst of futurity. To express this aspect of reality too, I have turned to the stories of the saints for imagery. In Connemara and the Burren as well as in Aran, generations of the pious and credulous have interpreted hundreds of little oddities of geology as traces of the saints, and my maps of these territories are discreetly asterisked with such miraculous sites, which I have gone to immense pains to locate and record. In one of the Aran Islands there is a spring well with curious indentations on its rim – prints of the hands of a voyaging saint who came ashore to drink at it. Near Cleggan in Connemara a head-shaped stone with red streaks of jasper in it marks the spot where a saint was beheaded, so giving the place its name (*cloigeann*, a head). At the top of a pass in the Burren are a holy thorntree and the marks of the knees of St Brigid, who paused there in her travels to look back prayerfully to her far-off homeland in Kildare. My literal incredulity liberates these spots of holiness from their footnote-like dependency on hagiography. As I said, within the world there are no miracles; in fact I believe that the only true believer in miracles is one who believes they do not happen. We should reserve the idea of such events, infinitely rare, impossibly free from the chains of cause and effect, to play the part of dazzling emblems of the potentialities hidden in any event whatsoever.

My maps are constellated in particular by holy wells, most of which would otherwise be known only to a few of the older inhabitants of their immediate localities. Many would read my devotion to these traces of popular, or formerly popular, faith as a symptom of religious cravings suppressed. Am I so blinded by the smoke of the factual I do not realize I am walking over the embers of my buried spirituality? If I have a religion (but I think the term does not fit my attitudes) it is one that burns through the ground I tread, from deeper in the Earth. Just as many of the so-called saints are artefacts of the Christianization of Celtic legends, ancestral heroes hastily kitted out with halos, so their holy wells are sites of pre-Christian earth-worship. This stratum of the sacred outcrops unusually frequently in the landscape of Ireland, even today; for instance, in the names of the country itself – in our address, once again.

It was on the eve of May, a Thursday, the 17th day of the moon, in the Year of the World 3500, that the ancestors of the Irish first set foot on the shores of Ireland. At that time the island was in the possession of the Tuatha Dé Danann, the 'people of the Goddess Danu', and the invaders soon met one of them, a lady accompanied by hosts of druids and magicians. She told them the country was named from her, Banba, and asked that it should always bear that name, which was agreed. Later they met a second lady, Fódla, and had the same conversation with her. Finally they met a third, Ériu. 'Warriors,' she said, 'Welcome. Your coming has been long prophesied. The land will be yours, and there is no finer island in the world. But grant that my name be on it for ever.' And they agreed. The only untoward note in the discussion came from one of the warriors, Donn, who said, 'Not to her do we give thanks for it, but to our gods and to our strength.' And the Goddess – for of course that's what she was – reproved him and foretold that neither he nor his children would profit from the land. All this we may read in the ancient *Book of Invasions of Erin.*

Nominally, each of these avatars of the Celts' triple Earth Goddess (as modern folklorists would identify them) has received her due, for Banba and Fódla were celebrated by the bards and figure as representations of the oppressed Gael in the vision-poems of the seventeenth century, and Ériu is of course Éire. But the implication of the curse on Donn is that if the land is taken by force the outcome will be sterility. I am acutely aware of the fact that cartography has historically been associated with conquest, colonization, control. The Ordnance Survey was a function of the army. Therefore I have taken care that the mapping I have been essaying for the last quarter-century or so in the west of Ireland be one that returns the territory mapped to itself, to its inhabitants, and that I hope is not subject to the reproach of Ériu.

This myth of the naming of Ireland accords with the fact that in Celtic society kingship was conceived of as marriage with the tutelary Goddess of the territory. Kings come and go, mere history; the land pursues its eternal and mysterious cycles. Under a just and integral king the realm prospers and is bountiful; under an unjust or maimed king it withers into a wasteland. With the triumph of Christianity the role of the Goddess necessarily became unofficial. In the Burren I came across her as the legendary Brónach Boirne, the sorrowful one of Burren, the Hag who haunts Lough Rask near Ballyvaughan. To Dermot O'Brien in the early fourteenth century, establishing his rule over what is now County Clare, she was a fairy lover; to his rival Donough O'Brien she appeared as a frightful banshee washing piles of heads and limbs in the lake and foretelling his death in battle.

Even today, the Otherworld having foundered into oblivion, these archaic patterns of thought, established perhaps before the role of the male in generation was realized, obtrude in our metaphors. We no longer believe in goddesses, but the stoutest atheists among us (among us men, perhaps I should say) cannot resist the identification of land with woman. J.M. Synge on his first visit to the Aran Islands in 1898, wrote 'With this limestone Inishmaan I am in love ... and hear with galling jealousy of the various priests and scholars who have lived here before me,' and flirted with the idea of marrying a woman who would personify the island. Following him some knowing generations later, I (or at least my subconscious) energetically feminized the island I was trying to capture in the cartographical net: 'Round and round the island form, round and round the furry tomb' went a ditty in a dream of that time, and my night-self was delighted with its subtlety in substituting tomb for womb. Recently an otherwise approving review of my essays on landscape and mapping, by Catherine Nash, a feminist cultural geographer, has pointed out the exclusiveness of my 'openly sexualised description of the resistances, climactic pleasures and exhaustion of fieldwork'. This is a matter I take seriously.

What is the role, nowadays, of this rumpled bed of a metaphor? Most trivially, it is a slightly disguised, displaced or sublimated sexual fantasy – but then mapping, especially in the west of Ireland, involves a lot of lonely hours crouched under inadequate bushes waiting for the rain to stop, and perhaps one may be forgiven such vaguely warming ruminations. More important is its gender-asymmetry. It seems only natural to associate by metaphor the land, or the earth as a whole, that brings forth and sustains its biota in accordance with rhythms as old as life itself, with the female of our own species. A metaphor is a bridge intended to carry meaning across from one topic to another – but as soon as the bridge is established, meaning will sneak across it in the other direction, unobserved. To think of the land as a woman is to strengthen an unthinking identification of woman with the autonomic side of her being, and her reproductive biology in particular. Also, if the territory is female, the explorer, the researcher, even the cartographer, that most circumspect of conquistadors, by the banal law of opposites, must be male – implying that the female is short of the necessary qualities of intellectual and physical adventurousness. But nowadays something approaching a fair proportion of the fieldworkers I depend upon for their specialist knowledge in researching my maps are women, which makes the underlying trope sound terminally oldfashioned. Further, mapping, in particular, has been historically the imposition of interpretations on the previously meaningless, the appropriation for covert and often exploitative purposes of the passive, empty, terrain; the consolidation of the mapper in this masculinist, colonial, role, can only thicken the mystique of objectivity in which the process is usually obscured.

To all these points I unreservedly subscribe. However, they do not exactly address the grounds for disquiet this essay is picking its way across. It may be that the imagery I have been discussing derives its power, pathos and persuasiveness from an illicit appeal to a supernaturalist mode of thought I reject. Liberating the saints and their miraculous wells from their rags of historicity, I use them as poetic expressions of the powers of nature – but does their relict sanctity infect my poetry with untruth? Is the idea of a sacred landscape still viable? The ascetically naked and tonsured hills of the Burren have been extolled for their spirituality. This resonant claim arose recently in the context of defending the Burren against the Irish State and its minions, who wanted to build an 'interpretative centre' in a particularly open and unspoiled part of it and bring in coachloads of tourists, which would have necessitated straightening the winding lanes and so on – a misconceived scheme which was heroically opposed by a local group for nine years and finally defeated in 2000. I supported the defenders of the Burren, but I feel they were ill-advised in conjuring up ad-hoc spiritual values. The Burren claims attention in its own right through its many singularities, not as a pointer to something transcending it. (Chartres is a spiritual building in that sense; it points metaphorically, as well as architecturally, to heaven.) If the Burren appears sometimes to be unearthly, that is because of the narrowness of our perspectives on the Earth. And if the Earth appears to revenge itself for our violations, as it may be doing already through global warming, it is as a self-adjusting system of feedback loops, not as a conscious being acting with intent. In trying to capture my feelings about the territories I have explored, I once described myself as 'a discriminating earth-worshiper'. But earth-worship itself is a sacrifice to an even deeper central fire, a universally immanent Deity, or that more subtle, distilled essence of it, the Divine, and these concepts are of no use to me either as explanations for whatever physics' latest Superstring Theory hasn't got tied up, or as lifebelts in the maelstrom of inexorable personal extinction, or as tokens of my many attitudes to this intriguing, stupendous and appalling world that for the time being includes me.

So, what I would like to find is a language for these questions, not dependent on personalizing the land, neither sexualizing nor spiritualizing my relationship with it. To date, all I have towards that is what I have written about in *Stones of Aran* and elsewhere, the act of walking. To me, walking is a way of expressing, acting out, a relationship to the physical world; there are of course many others, notably in art. This sort of walking is an intense cognitive and physical involvement with the terrain, close to but not lapsing into identification with it, not a mysticism; and not a matter of getting from A to B but of lingering, revisiting, cross-hatching an area with one's most alert and best-informed attention. And my maps are the lasting traces of such mobile reveries; they are drawn in footprints. Sometimes, looking back on the times they represent for me, I feel they have been dreamed in footprints.

There, for the time being, I stand. However, one more walk remains to be described …

★

One winter evening, cycling home from fieldwork in Inis Ní, as I passed under the great beechtrees that shadow the road just north of Roundstone, I heard a sound – axe, mallet, spade; I forget which, but one of the forthright notes of countryside handwork – from within the wood. The little demesne and the Victorian mansion hidden in it, once the home of the landlord's agent, now belongs to a consortium of nature-loving Dutch who at that time employed as their gardener a learned hermit, a philosopher, perhaps a mystic, or so I had heard. I left my bike at the gate and went in to find this curiosity.

John Moriarty looked much as he appears on the cover of one

of the strange treatises that he was to publish subsequently: large-framed, at one with the spade or axe or mallet he was shouldering, in an ancient workjacket of many pockets and a wide leather belt that gave him the figure of a Tolstoy. His big visage also had enough pockets for a lifetime's tremendous experiences, and was topped by a joyful explosion of grey curly hair. We talked, and as on many later occasions it took only a couple of introductory sentences to bring us to the One and the Many. Through a gap in the trees, Inis Ní appeared across the bay crystallized by the level rays of sunset; full of my findings, I named all its inlets and headlands and hillocks. John was admiringly receptive to this excursion into the Many, but his quest is interior. Some years earlier he had abandoned a university career in Canada (having looked up from the Keats ode he was expounding and realized how inadequate its assumptions were to the howling desert of snow filling the classroom window), and had returned to Ireland, supporting himself with odd jobs, searching for a place in which to purge his mind of its European culture and open it to the vastitude of the Divine. The intervening years had been of solitude, ascesis and near breakdown. But as I was to discover, his unremitting application to the working out of his vision is in no conflict with a fine sense of humour and a generous and inventive humanity.

On that occasion we each stood our ground, which according to me was on a certain planet, in such-and-such a country, county, barony, townland, and so definably on indefinitely, whereas for him this pyramidology of place was a pointless horror unless it ultimately rested on Divine Ground. Summing up, John felt that deep down we agreed; but I thought that this was typical of his metaphysical thirst for the One, and that in fact we disagreed, in accordance with my basic tenet that difference is the *sine qua non* of existence. As we parted, I remember, a huge full moon like a ripe peach floated up into a silk-green sky from the snow-dusted peaks of the Twelve Bens, and Connemara momentarily became a province of mystic Tibet.

After that John used to call in whenever he was in Roundstone for his frugal shopping, and we had many resounding arguments; one day M had to banish us from the kitchen because we were thumping each other over the head with the dreadful word 'epistemology' with such violence that the sauce she was preparing separated. On Sundays John would find M and me having breakfast in bed, sybaritically pillowed, and would take a seat opposite us, sip a cup of lukewarm water and hold forth about the Abyss until we began to feel it opening immediately at the foot of our bed. In those years he was compounding what seemed to me a bizarre synthesis of shamanism and Christology out of an exorbitant array of excerpts from all the world's myths; I was anxious to get a sense of the whole of this mighty work, and persuaded him to send his bulky typescripts, which he was convinced were unpublishable, to Antony Farrell at Lilliput Press, who had venturesomely undertaken my *Stones of Aran*. The result to date has been five tomes, *Dreamtime*, the trilogy *Turtle Was Gone a Long Time*, and the autobiographical *Nostos* – slow sellers, largely ignored by the literary sceneshifters, but defiantly existent, asserting their rights to shelf-space in futurity; in all, a noble act of publication against the grain. I have been called upon to review them two or three times ('Not more than 350 words – and please make it lively!') and have done my best to square my admiration for John's dedicated life and radiant spirit with doubts as to whether these writings adequately carry his genius, and my rejection of his points of departure and arrival (they are the same) with wonder at his gigantic circumambulation. Hence the well-hedged tribute I see has been quoted on the jacket of his latest volume: 'Even dissenters like myself can be grateful to John Moriarty, for he has gone farther up the front steps to heaven and down the back stairs to hell than most of us will ever dare.'

Then John left Connemara for distant Kerry, to our great loss. A year or so later I went to visit him there. He lives rather isolatedly within a panorama of mountains which includes a glimpse of just one of the Paps of Danu, Dhá Chích nAnann, a special object of veneration for him. Danu or Anu, the 'mother of the Gods of Ireland', is to be traced back through the Indo-European realm, appearing as Dôn the Welsh mother of wizards, reflected in the rivers Don, Danube and others, originating perhaps as the stream-goddess Danu of Sanskrit texts. On my journey down to Killarney, keeping a lookout to the left from the train window on John's instructions, I had already seen the pair of smooth and shapely hills, each with a prehistoric summit cairn as nipple, lovely as only breasts can be. The next day John took me for a walk to their vicinity, to rejoice in the return of his strength after long debilitation, and, as it transpired, to invoke the blessing of the Goddess on my topographical labours.

It was the height of summer. Being taken for a walk by John is like being taken for a walk by a mountain, and we strode out mightily, blown along by a gale of talk. Towards the end of a long straight lane through farmland we diverted from the direct approach to the Paps and took a loop around a little valley – *ag dul deiseal*, clockwise, sunwise, everything having to be done with ceremony – in order to visit a holy place known as the City Well, in old times a place of May Eve rituals and revelry. 'City' is a mistranslation of the Irish *cathair*, a ringfort, and its ancient name was

Cathair Chrobh Dearg, the 'fort of Red Claw'. Crobh Dearg is said to have been one of three sister nuns who are associated by folklore with fire in various ways. The chief of them, Latiaran, used to visit a forge every day to collect the 'seed' of the fire and carry it back to her cell in her apron. One day the smith complimented her on her pretty ankles, and in a moment of pride she looked down at them, whereupon her apron caught fire. Cursing the smith and prophesying that no smithy would ever flourish there in future, she sank into the ground and didn't come up again until she reached her cell, which she never again left in daylight, to avoid being a cause of sin in others. Crobh Dearg too vanished into the earth where her holy well now is, by the entrance to the Cathair. This strange name, 'Red Claw', hints that behind the three saintly nuns looms the triple Goddess in her destructive guise as Badhbh (the carrion crow), Macha and Anu, vengeful spirits who hover over battlefields and glut themselves on carnage.

The Cathair is a grassy space enclosed by a low circular rampart of lichen-covered stonework, within which one visits, pilgrim-wise, a number of crosses inscribed on rock outcrops and set slabs, some of them with a little depression like a navel at the centre to which rain and dew supply holy water. Opposite the entrance, therefore in the place of honour, is the standard blue-and-white statuette of the Virgin Mary, whose cult has been superimposed on that of the Celtic mother-goddess. As John made his 'rounds', running his thumb along the grooves of the crosses, widened by centuries of believers' thumbs, I hung about the entrance gate like a child dragged unwillingly to church, disapproving of John's reabsorbtion into the ranks of the pious, and sardonically noting the plastic rubbish lying around the holy well.

The day already seemed to have taken a wrong turning, and

was to worsen. When he came out, John told me that a little farm building nearby which had sheltered a Court of Poetry in the old days of poetic Kerry had been bulldozed recently. We walked up through the last of the fields to the commonage. There were no larks; the farmers' annual springtime burning-off of dead vegetation had seen to that. Mounds of stone and rubble had been dumped along the edge of the mountainside, and at the end of the track was the rusty corpse of a car. We took to the slope, and found ourselves treading across bare earth, cracked, greyish, with the texture of scar tissue. The hillside looked as if it had been burned, burned, burned, year in year out; it was the *tiere gaste* of Arthurian and Celtic legend, the land laid waste and accursed through the King's incapacity, which John interprets as our repression of Nature within and without us. We trekked across it in deepening depression. At the brow of the slope we left the burned-out area and trod into good deep heather in the little stream-valley coming down from between the Paps. Here John reverently took off his shoes; I did not. One more trial was to confront us: a fox stretched out across a tussock of heather as if basking in the sun, embalmed in the hyperreality of death, converted into an exact simulacrum of a fox, lifelike in every detail down to the shotgun pellets in it.

After that horror the journey improved. We climbed to the shallow ripply lake the stream spills out from, and picked our way around it to the beginning of the pass between the two hills. A grey and wind-raked mountain ash where the way begins to steepen marks the point beyond which John feels it would be presumptuous to go. Here, speaking out of this deep heart of the island of Ireland, he was to thank me for accomplishing the work it had been given me to do, and I could baulk and resile no longer. Clambering up to the tree, he reached out and grasped it by one of its many elbows, then stretched back his free hand for me to hang onto, the last link in the chain that would conduct the attenuated and therefore bearable shock of the Divine. I have to omit words here once again. They were, like all John's speech, generous, deeply considered, magniloquent, and I rejoice that at the last moment I was granted the good grace to receive them; but they are gone and the cliffs above have ceased to repeat them.

We heard a peregrine falcon's exultant shouting to its young far up on those cliffs as we turned away and began to follow the golden-brown stream in its tumbling descent. It was still only the middle of the afternoon when we reached the road and houses. A few people were leaning on their cars outside the school waiting for the children to come out; a man recognized John's face from a recent TV programme, and we stopped to talk. John told them where we had been. 'But we didn't go beyond the rowan tree,' he said, 'and do you know why?' – in the booming rhetorical mode he sometimes adopts to cover a shyness – 'Because it's holy ground!' The man inspected him for a moment, and then in a voice that gave no clue as to the presence or absence of irony, replied, 'There's a lot of holes in it, right enough.'

Which brought us down to earth again – the worn and torn old Earth through which shows, according to John, the Divine Ground, and according to me, nothing.

THE EXTREME EDGE

'In the high mountains of our fatherland there is a little village.' It lies in the middle of a wide valley, and at its centre is the church with its pointed spire. To the south rises a snowy peak, an object of pride to the villagers and of admiration to the occasional visiting climber or artist. A path from the village crosses a high neck or col between this peak and another, and leads to a little town in the next valley. The village shoemaker has brought the daughter of a wealthy dyer of the town back home as his bride. The couple have a boy child and then a girl, who at the period of this story (it is Adalbert Stifter's 'Bergkristall'; I came across it when trying to learn German once and it has remained with me as a puzzle and a challenge) are old enough to be allowed to take the path over the col to call on their grandparents. One Christmas Eve, the weather being fine, they are given permission to make the journey. On the way they find that a post marking the highest point of the pass has fallen, but this is of no consequence since they are so familiar with the route. Their grandmother and grandfather welcome and make much of them, but then, mindful of the shortness of these midwinter days, pack them off homewards early in the afternoon. As the children climb towards the col snow begins to fall, and they wonder if the post will be covered. Soon they are wandering in a 'white darkness'. The boy presses on like someone who feels he has to reach a turning-point, the little girl follows with perfect trust. Precipices rise on either side of them; they clamber among huge boulders of ice. When it is too dark to go on they creep into a house-like recess among piled rocks and they eat the food they find in the parcels their grandmother has given them to carry home. The boy insists that the little girl not fall asleep. The snow has ceased, the sky is clear and starry. They hear the glacier crack three times with a terrible sound as if the earth had broken in two. In the middle of the night they watch the sky fill with shimmering colours, 'a discharging of electrical tensions caused by the snowfall, or some other manifestation of nature's mysteries'. At dawn they set off again, but can find no way out of the ice fields. Then they see a red flag waving far off and hear a note from a shepherd's horn. Soon they are in the safe hands of searchers from the village, and are brought back to the pass, where a sleigh awaits them, and so home, with rejoicing. They have missed the ceremonies of Christmas Eve, the coming of the Christchild, but the girl is able to tell her mother that they saw Christ the Saviour during the night when they were sitting on the mountain. And when they have rested and recovered a little they are allowed to get dressed to receive the presents He has brought them.

So the story is brought softly down from perilous heights to a tender and pious domesticity. Stifter is regarded as the quintessence of the mid-nineteenth-century literary value-system rather derogatorily called *Biedermeier*, a bourgeois quietism, a universalization of propriety. According to his preface to *Bunte Steine*, the collection that includes this story, Creation is ruled by a 'gentle law', to which we can accommodate ourselves through stillness of mind. But one is left to feel that the outcome of the story could have been otherwise; the law of the ice fields is not usually gentle. Stifter meticulously describes both the topographical and the social setting of the incident in their unchanging consonance. But most of all he lavishes detail on the place – if it is a place – on which the story pivots, the summit of the pass. The wooden post marking it is called the *Unglücksaüle*, the accident-post or pillar of misfortune, and bears a picture of a baker who died there, which the children are delighted to be able to examine closely when they find the post fallen – not a mountaineer or a woodsman on his way to the upper slopes, but a baker, a representative of the community's warm, nurturing heart. It is to this ambiguous, treacherous, disconfirming spot that my mind, like the story, keeps returning.

The top of a pass is a strange specialization of nowhere, like a crossroads; it is nothing in itself but choice of ways and the possibility of going astray. The route from valley to valley, briefly ascending out of the everyday of life, drawing breath for a moment and then descending into it again, crosses another route that goes from peak to peak, clambering down dangerous slopes, striding out on an easy stretch, and mounting again into extremity. Around the saddle-point itself the lie of the land may be quite ambivalent; if visibility is limited there may be no clues from the trends of slopes as to which is the right way. Geometrically it is a point of zero curvature, where the curvature of the mountain route is cancelled out by the opposite curvature of the home route. Dynamically it is a point of unstable equilibrium; on a surface of this form, a ball could rest here but the slightest disturbance will send it rolling down one way or the other. Emblematically it is the destabilization of Stifter's tale and the certainties it propounds. (If these observations amount to a deconstruction of the story, they are not intended as an exercise in a criticism that prides itself on being deeper than its subject, but rather as exemplifying the fact that all true writing undermines itself, is deeper than itself. Were it not so, why would we attempt such writing? For we already know what we know, and hope always for more.)

Space sets its traps not only in the wild but in the most banal of places. Because I can only think through sensations and argue by memories, I'll recount a trivial and absurd incident from a time when I had a holiday job with a firm of office cleaners. Sometimes my mates and I had to work in the small hours scrubbing walls and ceilings in the deserted typing pools and corridors of international corporations. On one such occasion I happened to enter a huge washroom, a sterile neon-lit hall, symmetrical in layout, with a row of cubicles down each long wall, and down the centre a low partition with washbasins backing onto it on either side. The upper part of this partition was clad with mirror-glass, and as I crossed obliquely towards one of the basins I was probably half aware of my reflection approaching from the other side. Having washed my hands I glanced up at myself in the mirror – and there I wasn't! There were the taps, the basin, the tiled floor, the row of cubicle doors, but I myself was missing. It only took a moment for me to realize that the section of partition above this particular basin had for some reason been removed and that I was looking not into a reflection of my side of the room but into the real space of the other side. A minor contretemps (or *contre-espace*) – but it shook me, to see the mirror-image of my own body-world untenanted, to see absence grinning like a skull and saying, 'As I am, so shall you be!' – a mere prank of geometry, a reminder that space is compact of hiding-places in full view, ambushes in open ground, oubliettes under familiar floors. Although it is the framework of my being, and perhaps because it is such, I do not trust space an inch.

What the ultimate cause of my sense of the precariousness of space is I do not know; it feels as old in me as the ability to walk, although my life has been relatively cushioned and sheltered from falls. But I read it everywhere in what I write, in all those images of bilocation and existential twinning, of standing on the upturned soles of one's reflection in a calm sea, of groping blindfold across fissured crags. And I find it in others' writing, even where surely no such sense is intended; in fact I believe the origin of my imagery of the step, which informs the whole of *Stones of Aran* and which I sought to explicate in *The View from the Horizon*, is a misremembered passage in a rather obscure treatise, read in my usual snatching forgetful way when I was at university: *Foundations of Inductive Logic*, by the economist Roy Harrod.

Harrod's venture into philosophy, in the no-nonsense tradition of his heroes J.S. Mill and J.M. Keynes, aims to supply a sound basis for what one might call the unspoken working hypothesis of all our lives: 'the fact that things have been found in experience to be thus and thus gives, in and by itself, a valid reason for holding that they will continue to be thus and thus for the time being'. This 'Principle of Experience' can only give probabilities, not certainties, of things continuing 'thus and thus'. But, with this limitation, Harrod purports to show, by a neat bit of probability theory, that it is valid; also, that it is the basis of induction in general, i.e. the formation of general laws and expectations on the basis of observed instances. Whether he is successful or not is irrelevant here (I remember that A.J. Ayer reviewed the book positively even though he thought that a proof of the Principle of

Induction was neither necessary nor possible). What mattered to me were some scenarios Harrod used to illustrate his argument.

The general idea is that if one is experiencing some sort of continuity – whether it be a series of observations of a repeated event like sunrise, or a uniformity of colour or pattern in a surface – the latest instance of it is statistically unlikely to be the last, and this unlikelihood increases as the series continues:

> We are starting as we must in a fundamental analysis of induction, from a condition of total nescience. Before making any inductions, man could know nothing whatever, except what is under his nose. Consider a journey by such a nescient man along a continuity.... If one is journeying over an expanse, but in total ignorance of whereabouts on it one is, one is unlikely to be on the extreme edge of it.

And to clarify this notion of 'extreme edge':

> If in blind man's buff one finds oneself on the drawing-room carpet, it is not unlikely that one is within a yard of the extreme edge of it.... But if one has got lost in the Sahara Desert, one is not likely to be within a yard of its edge, for to be so would be to be on its extreme edge.

These likelihoods are to be understood in terms of frequencies:

> To say that 'we are unlikely to be on the extreme edge' means that if we continuously believe that we are not on its extreme edge, we shall certainly be right much more often than we are wrong; thus we shall certainly be right in deeming that we are probably not on its extreme edge. It is implicit in the meaning of 'probable' that we may none the less be on its extreme edge.

Out of this conjunction of blind man's buff, a desert wandering, and the almost obsessive repetition of 'the extreme edge', my mind put together a false memory. Until I dug the book out again recently I could have sworn that Harrod illustrated his argument with a dramatic and unnerving image of a blindfolded man walking on a bare cliff-edged plateau. Imagine oneself snatched out of the normal course of life and set down one knows not where, in utter darkness. Eventually one risks a step forward, out of one's perfect nescience, and finds firm footing. Another step, and then another, add to one's tentative belief that the ground underfoot, whatever its nature, is supportive. Each step is progressively less likely to bring one to the edge; in fact one comes to imagine that there may not be such an edge. Soon one is striding out confidently, towards the silently waiting precipice ... Thus, out of Harrod's offer of rational comfort for our thoughtless sense of security, I had fashioned a nightmare of insecurity.

I could find nominal support for such a perception of reality in Harrod, for in his concluding chapter I note this remark: 'Even what we claim to know must be taken for probable only; we may awake tomorrow to find that the reign of the vaunted laws of physics is over.... We wander about on our own little surface, pleased with our knowledge only because we cannot see the edge of its domain.' But this extrapolation beyond the empirical world leads him only into some rather bloodless speculations on truth, goodness, beauty and love, his rationalist-Anglican temperament paving the void beyond the edge with these sustaining categories. However, as he says, 'It is not inappropriate that there should be certain rites and places set aside and consecrated persons devoted to such speculation.' Perhaps religious places by their very form propose some comforting mediation between us wanderers and the beyond.

I explored this idea once when M and I, fleeing Connemara, were spending the hottest part of one summer in Aix-en-Provence. In temporary asylum from a countryside to which the great centuries of Christian architecture had dispensed only a handful of roughly-built oratories, we were savouring the grandeur, the elaboration, the sonority, of the city's churches. From the sky-lantern-lit cupola above the dim baptistery of the Cathédrale Saint-Sauveur we daily drank down great draughts of space. Looking up at the last of the sunset caught by the masonry of the Augustinian church climbing above the lamplit *place* where we were dining one evening, I thought of a knifeblade dug into *tapenade* or some other of those ochreous, Provençal taste sensations we were sampling for the first time. Leaning against a cool, shadowed wall and staring up at the midday-glorified tower of Ste-Esprit, I appreciated the high definition of the few trefoil handholds it offered for visual rock-climbing, relished its fierce, orange, materiality stamped out flat on a sky of azure, abstract, joy. These towers and spires do not point to the world above, but penetrate; they probe and sample space and light. From memories of the towers of Chartres shepherding the vast plain of La Beauce, and even from the spires of Kilburn, Neasden and Cricklewood glimpsed in my London rambles, which I used to identify with Proust's three church towers, I knew that in distant views they would be nodes and reference points in the fields of possible journeys, turning travel into pilgrimage.

Then, in 'Les Heures Lentes', a second-hand bookshop that approaches the ideal of such, run by a fragile, melancholy young lady and a massive black-and-white cat usually profoundly asleep in its window, which looks onto a shady little square crowded with café tables, I came across the indefatigably lugubrious rhetoric of Cioran. Opening his *La Tentation d'exister*, I found this:

> Contemplez les cathédrales: ayant perdu l'élan qui en soulevait la masse, redevenue pierre, elles se rapetissent et s'affalent; leur flèche même, qui

autrefois pointait insolemment vers le ciel, subit la contamination de la pesanteur et imite la modestie de nos lassitudes.*

How did that accord with my observations? I was enjoying the baroque theatricality of the side-chapels in Saint-Sauveur for its own sake, the gleams of gold in morbid gloom, the low secretive doors leading away into casuistical labyrinths, the unctuous swell of every form, the swaggering paunch of counter-Reformation Catholicism. But the phrase 'au siècle des siècles', 'ad seculae seculorum', recurring in the Masses we heard or overheard, moved me deeply. If it is the words of the cult, the constant and continuous repetition of its formulae over many generations and through an 'age of ages', that maintain the cathedral in existence, then without them the building, however well-preserved, is a ruin. And the question preoccupied me: What are cathedrals for, to us who do not sit by the smoky fire of religion?

If the cathedrals are to me primarily storehouses of space, height, darkness and light, and, externally, stone and sky and the sun's heat, then they are the exact opposite of what they are to the faithful: portals of a transcendent non-material world. What then distinguishes them from secular architecture or even from abstract sculptures? Letting them revert to (mere) stone, to stone for which one cares only aesthetically, would be a catastrophic waste of a millennial resource. But I can hardly call upon the persistence of sempiternal error to support my fleeting truth. Very approximately, and as a first guess: for me the cathedral consecrates the here-and-now, the instant, whereas for the believer it conserves

*Consider the cathedrals: having lost the *élan* that lifted up their bulk, become stone again, they shrink and crumple; even their spire, which in former times aimed insolently for the sky, submits to the contamination of heaviness and imitates the modesty of our lassitudes.

echoes of eternity. It would be easy to stray into spiritual mode and claim the consecrated here-and-now as being precisely an echo of eternity. But while I think that the universe may well be eternal I do not believe in Eternity, either in the form of the Life to Come, the Happy or Unhappy Ever-After, or as the ground, the metaphysical foundation stone, of temporal reality. So what does consecration mean? What do the cathedrals do, beyond the aesthetic, and the always more or less illusory and exploitative rooting, miring, of community in a century of centuries? An urgent question, connected with that of reappropriation (expropriation perhaps) of religious language.

Mozart's *Requiem* in the cathedral; an intent audience, every note crystalline. The vaults of the roof, with many additional vaultings of shadow, contrasting beautifully with the brightly lit stonework of the choir and its seven pointed windows. Looking up at the roof it seems suddenly I am looking up into my own skull, and it has vast room for unknown faculties, it is a mountain seen from within. The visible skeleton of Gothic makes it a corporeal style, an extension of ribcage, cranium, the acts of standing, balance, even walking (I think of the lines of columns, and the afternoon light processing from one to the next as the great doors are slowly opened behind us at the end of the concert). Gothic speaks to the skeleton in one's flesh, the lasting parts: spine, long-bones of arms and legs. The person potentially most conscious of this, most uplifted or crushed by it, must be the postulant prostrated at the intersection of nave and transept. Cathedrals intermediate between body and cosmos, magnifying the former and condensing the latter; they are interpreters between the two, or transformers, adapting the powers of each to the other. Or, echo-chambers giving our sense of self back to us from the walls of the world. When the organist attacks a mighty Passacaglia and Fugue as if intent on testing the building to destruction, sending inertial masses of air crashing from one end to the other of the biggest pipes, flinging treble notes around the vault like cataracts of shooting stars, even then the masonry holds, contains and returns to us praise and prayer, confirms our centrality in the structure of being.

For we are only talking to ourselves in such exchanges – even if to the deepest and most rarely addressed levels of ourselves – and we still have to face that which we cannot address and does not address us. Those cathedral-bottled oceanic surges bring me back again to a bleak, disconfirming, edge we lived near once, where, if one shouted, there was no echo because the space beyond was empty. Folklore of the Aran cliffs and those that have fallen from them mentions 'the step that isn't there'; if a step is a contract with the earth, this is the one the earth does not honour. Nevertheless one has to enter into such contracts at every moment, to continue in life. The clifftop is a natural emblem for extremal situations, actual or conceptual. One night in Aix I had some thoughts which at the time seemed to represent the uttermost reach of the human mind. I doubt I can recapture – not them, but the conviction of their reality and value. Not unusually for dream-thought, they concerned the inexpressible: what it is and why it is so. I risk banality in extracting them from the matrix of drowsy reminiscence in which I found them. I was back on the cliffs, listening to the seethe and crash of waves, hiss of rain, shriek of seabirds; or, trying not to listen, since listening implies selective attention and I wanted to be aware of the whole soundscape at once – barely possible in such a case, with such a spread of frequencies, hardly short of white noise, the summation of all frequencies. White noise is the absolute nadir of defeated expression,

expression defeating itself by accumulated self-interruption and auto-interference; hence the inevitable collapse of the attempt to express everything simultaneously, sound every note, play every tune. So the inexpressible is the All; it is not to be conflated with the Void, inexpressible only because there is nothing to be expressed. If the All is the Abyss, it is not Tohu-bohu or the quantum vacuum, formless source of all things, but the totality of possible forms. Expression entails selection and suppression, the gestalt and its background of absence. Hence the inexpressibility of the inexpressible. Nothing, no single thing, is inexpressible, but 'raids on the inarticulate' cannot bring home even a fraction of the totality of the expressible. And the reason for that is not just quantitative, as to what is to be expressed, the infinite overflow of subject-matter, but structural, as to expression itself. My metaphysics is sleepy, but in its sleep it clings to one of my few convictions. For a writer, on this interpretation, the cliff hangs over what cannot be written. Maybe one can gesture towards it with such strangely expressive words as 'inexpressible' and the mysteriously descriptive 'undescribable'; or one can enact it, as I have tried to do, exhausting myself in pursuit of inexhaustible possibilities, dancing on the edge. Perhaps that space beyond is visited by the mystic. In fact, it is tempting, the great circling fulmar-flight into the ineffable; but a profound distrust holds me back from it, a conviction that my task is here, guided by some such compass-rose as the little roundels of buckshorn plantain I find appressed to the ground on the very brink of Aran's cliffs.

There are, however, simpler and more basic interpretations, to restore a cutting edge to this soliloquy. The long cliff-sequence, the hundred pages of 'South' in *Stones of Aran*, can be read as a meditation on death. A thought of suicide, suppressed from that book, could find its place in the section called 'Perdition's Edge'. Occasionally when we were in wintry mood M and I would visit it – climbing the barren hill to the prehistoric cliff-fort of Dún Aonghasa, skirting its gloomy walls and following the windy clifftop a hundred yards farther west to a projecting angle called Carraig an Smáil, which an island author used to render as the Rock of Perdition. We knew what waves would be thundering against the wall of rock below on such a day, having watched them often and intently on lower shores; they bulge, burst, spout, gape and founder so individually one could give each a proper name – Stag-head, Sloppy Jim, The Walrus, Seven Hills, Hullabaloo – wave after wave, hour after hour, day after day. But from this height all that flux of identity was abstracted by distance into a slow regular hammering. We would lie face down on the almost bare stone of the clifftop and work our way forward until our heads stuck out over the appalling drop like gargoyles from a cathedral's eaves. But this was the anti-cathedral, the smithy of natural law; all things are on the anvil, they shall be thus and thus. Each blow shook the land and was transmitted to our frail soft bodies. Our minds too were shaken. After a time, immeasurable although perhaps brief, we would withdraw, reshaped, annealed, and take ourselves dizzily homewards, our personalities temporarily in a vanishing perspective.

If such a cliff can be a renewal, it is because it is also a means, invitation and temptation, to end one's life. Just four and a half seconds, I calculate, would separate – by what sublime panic? – the last step on earth from obliteration of the self. Believing that the right to one's own death is essential to one's personhood, however its exercise is subject to individual and communal obligations, I should find it possible to discuss ways and means in a usual tone. To throw myself off the cliffs that I have written up at such length would be fitting, to the point of melodrama. But nobody thereafter would be able to read me unconstrained by a fateful commentary; I would have permanently conditioned the reception of my work, at least until the reading world had forgotten either or both of it and me. Then there are the practicalities. It is a strenuous climb to this point, or would be for one suffering terminal illness, terminal sorrow; this is no death for the dying. Also, the kindly folk of Gort na gCapall would inherit the horrible task of finding and retrieving the ruins of my body. And, even if I got so far, exhibited such life-powers, could I nerve myself to the act? I have imagined it and dreamed it too often. The rollers curve in and are reflected back from the cliff with the regularity of balance-wheels, escapements, ratchets; I am falling into the teeth of the world's clockwork.... At what should have been the last, or nearly the last, moment, flesh and bone would wrench themselves away from the edge, and I would creep home to shameful continuance of life.

What strange relativity is this, that one sees another's last years as decline, whereas to the person who treads it with such effort the way is uphill, the ground ever steeper, the breath ever shorter. Finally there is no more ground, no more breath. If one could then come down from that painfully attained summit like a triumphant mountaineer, to admiring toasts and a well-paid lecture tour! But one cannot share this lonely heroism, though it is written into the genes of all mortals, or even savour it in solitude, for clouds of forgetfulness and bewilderment close in. There is not even a view to reward the climber, neither a panorama of the biographical archipelago nor an upwards vision of eternity; consciousness constricts itself into bone-ache.

No, of course, with luck, with love, with forethought, it may not, need not, come to this. Part of my forethought has been this deathly and unrealistic fantasy of the cliff. But if it is not to be the cliff, discussion of it is not matter for this book, and so I leave it. May it go easily, the untwisting of the threads of my life, and of that other life braided into mine! I am very much afraid of it.

CONSTELLATION AND QUESTIONMARK

The Mystic Hexagram

Pascal, before I opened biographies, was chiefly known to me for three pronouncements: his wager on salvation, his confession of cosmic agoraphobia, and his theorem. The first – 'If God does not exist, one will lose nothing by believing in him, while if he does exist, one will lose everything by not believing' – is unworthy of both God and human. The second, a mere whisper – 'Le silence de ces espaces infinis m'effraie' – still rattles the windows of civilization, and I shall follow its echoes in another essay. The third is this:

> *If a hexagon is inscribed in a conic, the points of intersection of its opposite sides will lie in a straight line.*

Ever since I came across it, in my first year at Cambridge, it has been my paradigm of mathematical beauty. When I go now to refresh my memory of its proof in a little textbook of projective geometry that has followed me around since then, I find a hole from which the relevant diagram has been cut out, reminding me that I used it (in those pre-photocopier days) to illustrate an article I wrote for a college magazine. I suspect that my jejune reflections on abstract art, maths and Eastern calligraphy would not have been accepted for publication had I not also been the editor; but one point from the essay comes in handy here. The geometrical air of some modernist art (I was thinking of my hero Mondrian, and Gabo and Hepworth among others) might lead one to suppose that the beauty of such works is in some way dependent on the beauty of mathematics; however, descriptions of them as geometrical configurations would not be of much interest to a mathematician. Conversely, the diagram exemplifying a theorem may or may not be beautiful, but the beauty of the theorem itself derives from invisible considerations such as the richness of connections it reveals among different mathematical ideas, its 'seriousness'. I borrowed this term from G.H. Hardy's *A Mathematician's Apology*, that high-minded extension of the Bloomsbury ethos to mathematics. Hardy further analyzes a theorem's 'seriousness' as dependent upon its 'generality' or relevance to a wide but well-discriminated body of ideas, and its 'depth', by which he seems to mean something like its explanatory power in the hierarchy of concepts. Nowadays I can recognize that my mathematical preferences are influenced by less purist factors as well: in this instance by the association of the theorem with Pascal's fast-burning lifestory, and indeed with the sound of his name, which promises both Gallic grace and passionate intellectuality.

In the language of geometry a hexagon need not be the sort of honeycomb-cell shape we call by that name in daily life; any six points joined into a circuit by six lines constitute a hexagon, even

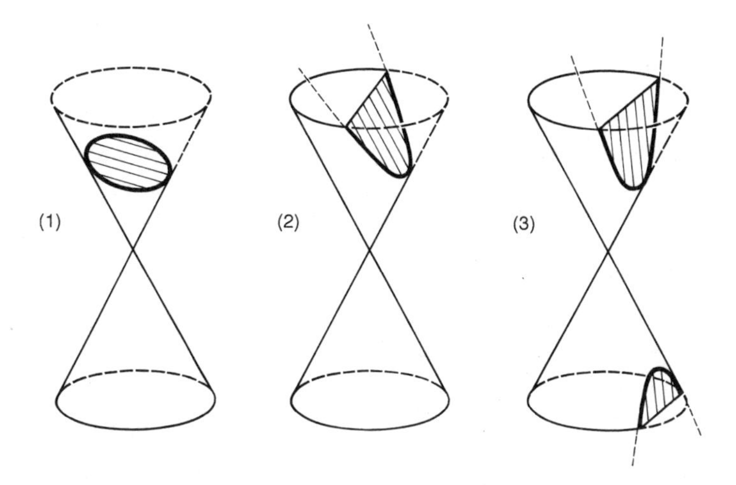

Figs. 1–3. Cross sections of the cone: (1) the ellipse; (2) the parabola; (3) the hyperbola. Only the central portion of the cone is shown; a complete cone has two 'branches', each of which extends to infinity. In (3) the cross-section cuts both branches, and so the hyperbola also has two branches.

if the lines cross one another. (I will say simply 'line', instead of specifying each time a straight line.) A conic (or conic section) is any of the curves obtained by taking a cross-section of a cone (Figs. 1-3). The circle is the simplest of them, and the others are familiar presences to those who read by night: the ellipse of light cast on the ceiling from the circular aperture in the top of a tilted lampshade, and the lovely and evocative shape it projects onto a nearby wall, elegantly rounded below and fading away upwards with the grace of an angel's wing until clipped by the ceiling – a parabola if the two limbs of the illuminated area would eventually become parallel, part of a hyperbola if they would diverge forever. Pascal's theorem, then, is a powerful generalization, covering any of the endless variety of hexagons that can be inscribed in a conic of any type or size. A watertight proof of it, starting from the basic definitions and axioms of lines and their intersections, is lengthy and involved. But one can almost *see* that it must be true, by looking at a few examples, starting with a very simple case: Take six points evenly distributed around a circle, A, B, C, D, E and F, and join them up in this order: ADBFCE and so back to A (Fig. 4). Calling AD the first side, the side opposite to it is the fourth, FC, and they intersect in X. The second side is DB and it intersects the fifth, CE, in Y. Finally the third side, BF, intersects the sixth, EA, in Z. Then, the diagram being perfectly symmetrical, it is obvious that X, Y and Z lie on a straight line.

Now join up the same six points in another hexagon thus: ADEFCB and back to A (Fig. 5). This time, to find the intersection of opposite sides DE and CB, for instance, we have to extend them. But, once again, from symmetry, the three crucial points (as I will call them) lie on a line. And a few experiments with less symmetrical hexagons will convince one that the theorem is certainly true for circles (Fig. 6).

Next, imagine any such diagram of a hexagon in a circle being constructed out of strings stretched across that aperture in the top of a lampshade. The doctored lampshade will throw a shadow diagram onto a wall or ceiling, showing a hexagon of some sort inscribed in a conic of some sort – and, since the shadows of straight lines are themselves straight, the crucial points in that diagram will lie in a line (Fig. 7). Surely enough examples have been exhibited to convince reason that Pascal's theorem is a general truth? Proving it – proving that there are no exceptions – is of course another story. (Pascal did so at the age of sixteen.) A complication arises if two opposite sides are parallel, but they can be considered to meet at infinity; if all three crucial points are infi-

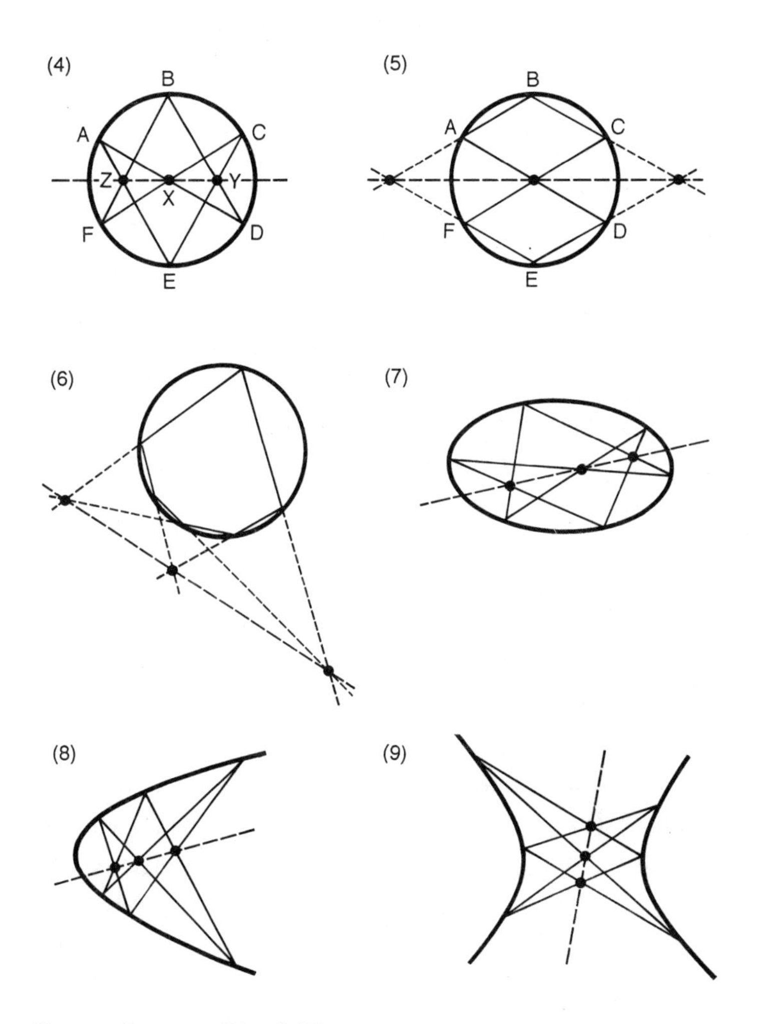

Figs. 4–9. Instances of Pascal's Theorem.

nitely far away, one can take them to lie on a conceptual 'line at infinity' – or one can ignore such anomalous cases, infinity being one of the more easily ignored aspects of the world.

I have deliberately surrounded this theorem with images of lamps projecting pools of light and of shapes projecting shadows. Pascal's is one of many theorems that survive projection; the conic may have its shape altered (a circle may become a parabola, for instance, as in Fig. 8), the sides of the hexagon may become longer or shorter and its angles larger or smaller, but the crucial points will still lie on a line. But most of the theorems in Euclid do not remain true under projection. The theorem that the two tangents from a point to a circle are equal, for example; project a diagram of it obliquely, and the circle will become an ellipse and the two tangents unequal. In general, distances and angles are changed by projection, but Pascal's theorem makes no mention of them; it belongs to a stratum of geometry more basic (deeper, in Hardy's sense) than the geometry of distances and angles.

Frustratingly, it is not known how Pascal proved his theorem. The result was announced without proof in 1640 in his first published work, a leaflet which is hardly more than an advertisement for a proposed treatise, circulated among the scientists of the day including Huygens, who forwarded it immediately to Descartes. After some basic definitions Pascal states two lemmas, of which the first is his theorem, for the case of a circle. (It is not in the trenchant and symmetrical form he later gave the result, and the hexagon is not explicitly mentioned, but the result is equivalent to what we now call Pascal's Theorem.) From these he proposes to show that the same is true of any conic section, and thence deduce all the elements of conics, including the subject's basic theorem, due to his elder contemporary Desargues, to whom he almost over-modestly acknowledges his debt: 'I owe the little I have discovered on this topic to his writings, and … I have tried to imitate his method, so far as was possible for me.' There was a certain rivalry between Descartes' algebraic approach to geometry and Desargues' more intuitive and visual methods, and perhaps this made Descartes read too hastily, for he mistakenly jumped to the conclusion that the youngster had not done more than imitate Desargues; later on he came to appreciate Pascal's genius, and was especially interested in his experiments on vacuums or '*la Vide*'.

From the correspondence of Pascal's mathematical mentor Père Mersenne later in 1640 we learn that Pascal deduced four hundred corollaries from his theorem, covering the field of Apollonius's treatise, the ancient classic on conics, and that the work was to be published in the following year. Desargues himself followed its progress, and referred in his own writings to 'this great proposition called *la Pascale*'. However, although Pascal published work on other branches of mathematics (and designed and built the first calculating machine), the promised *Traité des coniques* never appeared. When Fermat, with whom he had corresponded on and effectively co-founded the theory of probability, wrote to him in 1660 suggesting a meeting, he replied with expressions of esteem for 'Europe's greatest geometer' ('geometer' here meaning 'mathematician'), but sickness and his increasingly demanding religiosity reduced him to the saddening admission, 'I would not take two steps for geometry … I am engaged in studies so far from that turn of mind I scarcely remember what it is about.' We are all the losers by Pascal's miscalculated wager on God.

After his early death Pascal's manuscripts on conics were sent by his family to Leibniz, a great admirer, whose own achievement in founding what we now call analysis or calculus owed much to Pascal. Leibniz sorted them out into five treatises, had a copy made of the first, and returned them with a letter summarizing their contents, concluding by stating that 'This work is in fit state to be printed, and there is no question that it merits it.' Unforgivably, the family did not act on this advice. The manuscripts were seemingly deposited with Pascal's other papers at Saint-Germain-des-Prés, and are now lost. One feels like demanding that all the archives in which they could possibly be lying suspend all other business while they turn themselves inside-out like sacks to find them. As it is we have Leibniz's copy of the first treatise and his letter, from which it appears that the second treatise contained the proof of the theorem Pascal himself called the 'Hexagramme mystique', the consequences of which were elaborated in the subsequent treatises. The penetrating luminosity of the first treatise gives one a heightened sense of what is lost.

In the leaflet of 1640 the theorem is first stated for a circle, and then extended to the general conic. It seems clear that Pascal's method of doing this was to be by projection. In the first treatise he gives his definition of a cone, which amounts to this: if a line is drawn through a point on a circle and another fixed point not in the plane of the circle, then as the first point is allowed to move around the circle, the line sweeps out the surface of a cone (Fig. 10). And he deduces the properties of the various conic sections from those of the circle, by imagining that the eye is placed at the vertex of the cone, so that the conic is the image of the circle; i.e. points of the conic coincide visually with those of the circle. (This eye is highly idealized; it sees in all directions.) Leibniz, it appears from his private notes, was surprised and seduced by this 'optical method of cast shadows' and wondered if it could not 'transcend the cone and rise to higher considerations', that is to a general projective geometry not limited to lines and conics, which of course has come to pass.

In its origins, then, projective geometry relates to the theory of perspective and to the Enlightenment's fascination with the new tools of vision, the telescope, the microscope, the camera obscura, and so to the ocular imagery pervading the thought of that time, including Descartes' foundational doctrine of 'clear and distinct ideas' and even his conception of the relationship of soul to body. Later in his life Pascal composed an emblematic 'device' for himself, showing an eye surrounded by a crown of thorns. In the daytime world of fact and history, this commemorated 'the Miracle of the Thorn', an important event in the turbulent history of Port Royale, the Jansenist abbey with which his family was closely connected: a precious relic, a fragment of a spine from Christ's crown of thorns, had been lent to the abbey, and Pascal's niece had been cured of a dreadful fistula or ulcer of a tear-gland by application of the reliquary containing it; the occurrence was investigated by doctors of the Sorbonne and officially declared miraculous. But one could point to other connections, not figuring in the Cartesian realm of clear and distinct ideas, between this discomforting image of the eye surrounded by thorns, and that of the eye at the vertex of a cone, at the origin of the generators of form in general and of the mystic hexagram in particular.

The standard proofs of Pascal's theorem in today's textbooks use analytic or projective techniques that were not available in his time, or that seem foreign to his ocular and intuitive methods. However there is one proof, discovered in 1826, that uses only the simplest and clearest consequences of a few basic and strikingly visual ideas. Its inventor was Germinal Dandelin, a military engineer in Napoleonic France, and later professor of mining engineering in Brussels. Hardy, in trying to locate the aesthetic qualities of a proof, as apart from the 'seriousness' of the result, writes:

... there is a high degree of unexpectedness, combined with inevitability and economy. The arguments take so odd and surprising a form; the weapons used seem so childishly simple when compared with the far-reaching results; but there is no escape from the conclusions. There are no complications of detail – one line of attack is enough....

Dandelin's proof has all these narrative strengths. It is very dramatic; it sets off in an apparently irrelevant direction, appears momentarily to be lost in a thicket of lines, and suddenly confronts one with the result. I will expound it here, not for its own sake but, if I can, to convey the experience of understanding a proof, the rush of aesthetic adrenaline at its success. (To be realistic, perhaps that thrill will only be vouchsafed to those readers who have already trod similar ways, or are prepared to force their way through the thicket several times, to and fro, beating a path in which they will not be snagged by details. As for the others, I would rather they turn the page than abandon me completely!)

We will introduce a few preliminary ideas. (I note that mathematicians, including Pascal, frequently use this 'we', not because they count themselves kings of infinite space but that they are counting on, imploring, the reader to join with them in the venture, to share in the process of proof, which is nothing if it is not followed, and not in blind faith but with a critical mind ready to disconfirm or confirm it. A proof is a rational seduction. Also I should admit that I will glide over some little complications in the following, concerning lines that might be parallel rather than intersect; but anyone who has enough geometry to notice these elisions will also be able to fill them in. So, I beg you, follow me and if there are difficulties, jump over them without letting them perturb you.)

In Pascal's definition of a cone we have already met the concept of a line that sweeps out a surface. Dandelin's proof uses another form generated by lines, called a hyperboloid of one sheet. Imagine a sphere that can spin on a vertical axis; let a line be fixed to it, touching it at one point on its equator; then if the line is also vertical it will sweep out a cylinder when the sphere is rotated (Fig. 11). But if the line is askew it will sweep out the shape we need (Fig. 12). We will call its successive positions the generators; they are straight lines lying in this curved surface. (It is a common shape for lampshades because it can be made out of strings, playing the role of generators, stretched slantwise between two round loops of wire.) An equally askew line leaning in the other direction would sweep out the same surface, so there are two families of generators. No two generators of the same family intersect, but each generator of one family intersects all those of the other family.

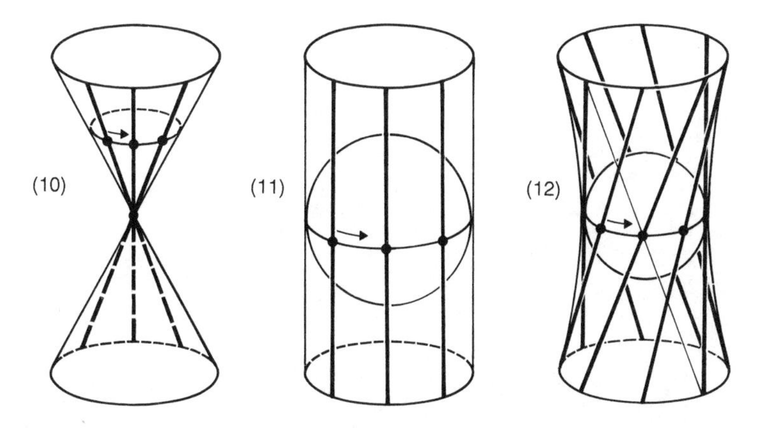

Figs. 10–12. Curved surfaces generated by movement of a line. A few generators are shown in each case. (10) the cone; (11) the cylinder; (12) the hyperboloid of one sheet, with some generators of the first family shown as bold lines and one generator of the second family as a fine line. (If the generators were extended far enough, the one from the second family would eventually intersect with all those from the first family, with the exception of the one directly opposite it, to which it is parallel.)

Having introduced the hyperboloid and its generators all we need are some obvious facts about lines and planes, such as that two intersecting lines define just one plane in which they lie, that two planes intersect in a line, and three planes in a point; for instance, the ceiling and two walls meet at the corner of a room.

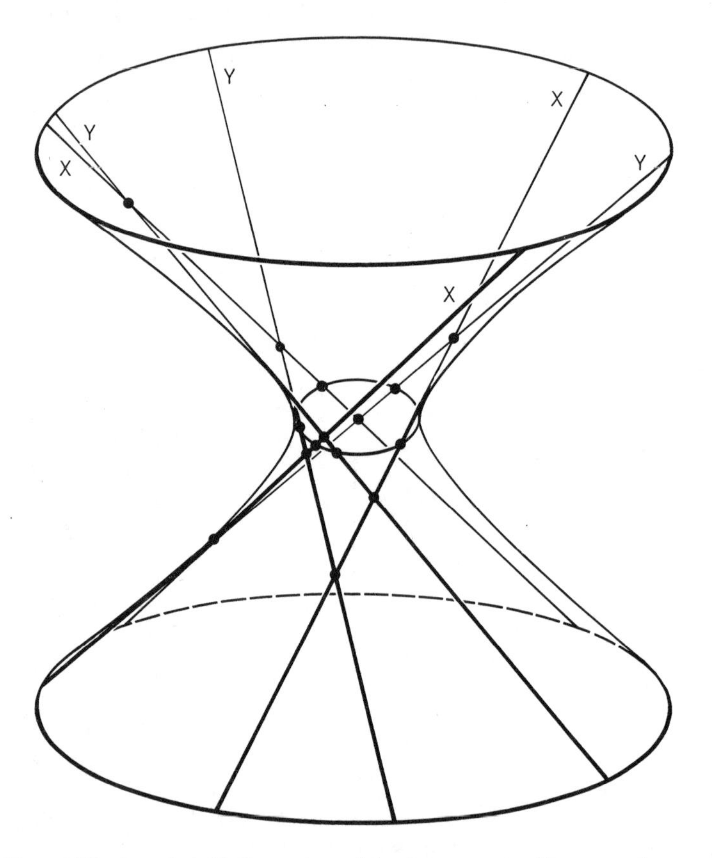

Fig. 13. The hyperboloid, the conic, and the six generators. (For convenience I have drawn the conic in the neck of the hyperboloid, but it could be in any position. Generators are shown by finer lines where they lie on the farther side of the hyperboloid. Generators of one family are marked X and those of the other family Y.)

Now we will take a plane cutting through the hyperboloid; if the plane is horizontal the intersection will be a circle, and if slanting, one of the other conic sections (this is easily proved, but we shall take it as established). In the conic we will inscribe a hexagon. Through one of its corners we draw a generator belonging to one of the families, through the next corner a generator from the other family, and so on all the way round (Fig. 13). That makes three generators from either family; each generator from one family meets the three from the other, giving nine points of intersection in all. Those first two generators and the first side of the hexagon make a triangle we will call the first triangle; each side of the hexagon has a corresponding triangle, so that the conic is encircled by six triangles (Fig. 14). (Is this a prefiguration of that eye crowned with thorns? If so it is a Pascalian 'reason of the heart' for believing that this proof is indeed the one used by Pascal.) Among the nine points of intersection mentioned are one corner from each of the six triangles; that leaves three more points of intersection, making a triangle we will call the seventh triangle.

Now look at the first triangle and the one associated with the opposite side of the hexagon, i.e. the fourth triangle (Fig. 15). Each of these triangles lies in a plane defined by two generators, and those two planes meet in a line, which is a side of the seventh triangle. That line meets the plane of the original hexagon, in a point we will call the first crucial point. But the two sides of the hexagon we have been concerned with, lying in the planes of the first and fourth triangle, must meet where those two planes and the plane of the hexagon all meet; that is, in the first crucial point. Similarly, each pair of opposite sides of the hexagon gives rise to a crucial point. These three points all lie in the plane of the hexagon and in the plane of the seventh triangle; so they must lie on

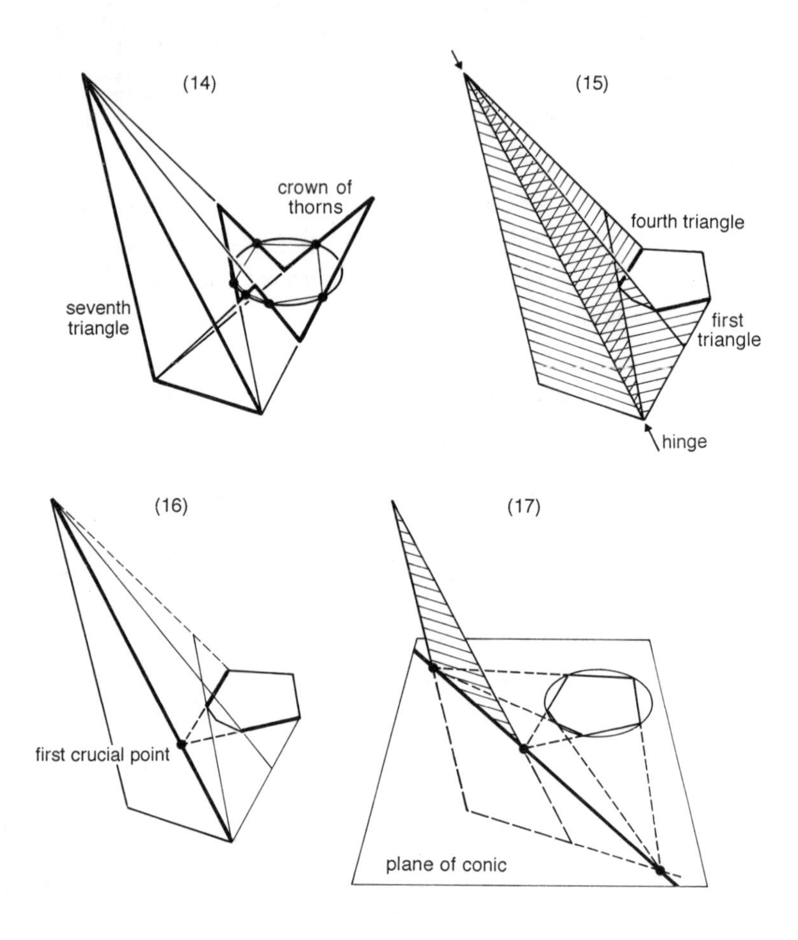

Figs. 14–17. Dandelin's proof. (Having established the configuration of six lines and their nine points of intersection, we can throw away the hyperboloid.) (14) The crown of thorns and the seventh triangle. (15) The planes of the first, fourth and seventh triangles all hinge on one side of the latter. (The conic is omitted for the moment.) (16) The crucial point where the first and fourth sides of the hexagon meet lies on the side of the seventh triangle. (17) All three crucial points lie in the plane of the seventh triangle, and in the plane of the hexagon; therefore they lie on the intersection of these two planes.

the line in which those two planes intersect (Fig. 17). Hence, '*La Pascale*': the intersections of opposite sides of a hexagon inscribed in a conic lie on a line.

It was not until the mid-nineteenth century that projective geometry's independence of and logical anteriority to our familiar schoolbook geometry was established. Euclid's geometry is 'metric'; the concept of distance is basic to it, and is left undefined within it. Projective geometry starts from hardly more than points, lines and planes, of which all we know is that two points define one line passing through them, two lines (lying in the same plane) intersect in one point, two planes intersect in a line, and so on. Obviously, since Pascal's definition of a cone mentions the circle it has a secret dependence on the idea of distance, a circle being the locus of a point at a fixed distance from another point, its centre. The same is true of Dandelin's proof above, since it utilizes the hyperboloid which was introduced with the help of a sphere. So these are not purely projective proofs, and it was some time before projective geometry found its own way to these theorems without such borrowings from metric geometry. But once the concepts of projective geometry have been sufficiently elaborated through theorem after theorem, the idea of distance can be defined in terms of them. Stranger still, the details of the definition can be chosen so that the metric geometry that arises is not the familiar one of blackboards; it can be the geometry that describes the properties of figures drawn on a curved surface such as that of a saddle or (with some massaging of difficulties) a sphere. These are all two-dimensional geometries – but three-dimensional projective geometry similarly gives rise to three-dimensional metric geometries analogous to those of the saddle-shape, the sphere, or the intermediate case of the flat surface. The three-dimensional equivalent of this last is the one we know, or think we know, as the Euclidean geometry of everyday life. But the others are logically consistent, if difficult to visualize; these strange ideas of curved spaces were given definite content by geometers of the nineteenth century building on the work of Pascal and his contemporaries. So how do we know what sort of space we actually live in? Perhaps if we could see more of it or measure shapes in it more accurately, we would find that on a cosmic scale it is spherical and returns upon itself like a circle or the surface of the globe. Or it may be an infinite space of the sort that terrified Pascal, in which case it is either flat (Euclidean) or hyperbolic (which is quite unimaginable in three dimensions, but a hyperboloid surface gives a two-dimensional inkling of its twisted nature).

What shape is space? And, as it is known to be expanding, will it continue to do so, or will it someday begin to contract again, perhaps into the state it started from, something hardly more than a point? These are the most enormous, if least pressing, of empirical questions, and I am exhilarated by the fact that our age is the first with the technical wit to answer them. In 1999 astronomers analyzing the motions of distant galaxies and the brightness of supernovas announced (with due tentativeness) their long-awaited findings: spacetime is either flat or very nearly so, and will expand at an accelerating rate for ever. Consider what this means: since the universe came into existence a finite length of time ago, its past is as nothing, quite literally, in mathematical terms, in comparison with what is to come. More marvellous yet, this will always be the case. Even if we ourselves perish in its cold, and Pascal's lamplight fades, the world is eternal dawn.

The Battleground of Form

But, should the universe prove the astronomers wrong by bringing itself to a full stop and disappearing, and even had it never existed at all, Pascal's theorem would still be true. Had no mind ever conceived a conic and no hand ever drawn a hexagon, it would still be the case that, 'If a hexagon is inscribed in a conic, the points of intersection of opposite sides will lie on a line.' The truths of mathematics transcend the existent, and by their own account of it mathematicians have to make strange journeys to bring those truths home to us; they talk of dream, revelation, intuition, and they claim to waste little time trying to prove results that later turn out to be false; they have a nose for the genuine article of faith. The logical processes of proof may have little to do with this primary capture of truth; after the event, it may be the labour of years to construct a proof others can follow.

My own capabilities in this regard are modest; Cambridge judged correctly in awarding me a second-class degree, and since I left the field I have forgotten most of the standard results and ready-to-hand techniques that are second nature to the professional. But I have had glimmers of illumination; in the days when I was a visual artist now and again an odd little theorem would turn up in my preliminary workings for an abstract painting, like a freebie toy in a cornflakes packet. And though my head is bloodied against the bars of my limitations I delight in following the creative mathematician so far as I can into that glorious unknown, which I picture not as a chill Platonic heaven but an Aladdin's cave, a darkness full of dazzlement. But are there cracked bowls and counterfeit jewels among its treasures? Are the mathematicians right in supposing that the goods to which they have their mysterious access are all sound? Sometimes it takes generations to come to a judgement on particular cases.

During my London years, since no one bought my artworks, I had to help support myself and my painting habit by drawing diagrams for technical books. One day in 1968 a typescript by a G. Spencer Brown* arrived from the publishers Messrs George Allen & Unwin, with the author's rough sketches to guide me in illustrating it. *Laws of Form* was the take-it-or-leave-it title. The meat of the text began with:

> THE FORM
>
> We take as given the idea of distinction and the idea of indication, and that we cannot make an indication without drawing a distinction. We take, therefore, the form of distinction for the form....

and it culminated with what appeared to be a derivation of the basic rules of logic from two drastically simple formulae. The steps in between looked like no mathematics I had ever come across; for instance:

$$\overline{\overline{\overline{\overline{a\,|}\,|}\,|}\;\overline{\overline{a\,|}\,|}\,|} \quad = \quad ,$$

according to which something rather complicated equals a blank. I was intrigued, and read it closely, following through the argument line by line, and came to believe that despite the Age-of-Aquarius tone of some of its pronouncements ('A recognisable aspect of the advancement of mathematics consists in the advancement of the consciousness of what we are doing, whereby the covert becomes the overt. Mathematics is in this respect psyche-

*For later editions the author hyphenated his name, as Spencer-Brown.

delic.') this was hard-hat mathematics, with genuine applications to electrical engineering, and that it did actually found logic on the formal properties of the elementary act of drawing a distinction.

Laws of Form uses the symbol $\overline{}|$ to mark a distinction; one could use a closed box just as well since it makes a distinction between its inside and its outside, but Spencer-Brown's mark is typographically handier. An innovative if unnerving move is to use a blank to represent the state of affairs before a distinction is drawn. A distinction allows us to name the states or values distinguished. Drawing the same distinction twice is no more informative than drawing it once; if a name is called and then called again, it still indicates the same state; so:

$$\overline{}|\,\overline{}| = \overline{}| \;.$$

The mark can be understood as an instruction to cross the boundary, say from inside to outside. Crossing the boundary again takes you back to your first state, or, 'to recross is not to cross'; Spencer-Brown writes this as:

$$\overline{\overline{}|}| = \quad .$$

(The two marks are drawn slightly separated for clarity, but should be thought of as occupying exactly the same position.) These two equations are the 'primitive equations' of a very simple arithmetic, in which there are only two elements, a mark and the absence of a mark. By applying these equations repeatedly it is possible to work out whether more complicated arrangements of marks within marks, such as that on the previous page, are equivalent to a single mark or to the absence of a mark.

So a calculus – that is, a symbolic system within which calculations can be made – is born. Within a few pages it flowers into theorems of some complexity. Very soon one can draw conclusions about unspecified arrangements of marks; if the letter p stands for such an arrangement, it is easily proved that

$$\overline{\overline{p}\rceil\; p}\rceil \;=\; \qquad .$$

(This follows from the fact that any arrangement is equivalent to $\overline{}\rceil$ or to $\quad$.) Not quite so simple, but provable in the same way, is the equation:

$$\overline{\overline{pr}\rceil\;\overline{qr}\rceil}\rceil \;=\; \overline{\overline{p}\rceil\;\overline{q}\rceil}\rceil\; r \;.$$

Already the arithmetic has developed into an algebra, with these two equations as its primitive propositions. Now we jump to another level of considerations with endless arrangements such as

$$f \;=\; \overline{\overline{\overline{\overline{\ldots a}\rceil\, b}\rceil\, a}\rceil\, b}\rceil \;,$$

where the string of dots indicated that the same pattern continues indefinitely. We can write this as

$$f \;=\; \overline{\overline{fa}\rceil\, b}\rceil$$

and say that f is re-entered into itself. Equations of this sort can have two solutions; for instance

$$\overline{\overline{f}\rceil}\rceil = f \;,$$

whether $f = \overline{}\big|$ or $f = \quad$.

An obstacle, i.e. a spur to invention, then arises:

$$f = \overline{f\,}\big|$$

does not work for either of the standard values of *f*. Whatever the value of *f*, the equation contradicts itself; it has the structure of a paradox. Spencer-Brown proposes to call the value of *f* imaginary in such cases. (Analogously, in the algebra of numbers, when we come to an equation like $-1/x = x$, which is not satisfied by any real number, we invent the so-called 'imaginary' number *i*, defined as a solution of that equation. It is routine in both pure and applied mathematics to use such imaginary numbers in calculating results represented by real numbers.) Or we can imagine a tunnel undermining the distinction which up to now has been inviolate (Fig. 18), and picture the value of *f* flowing outwards,

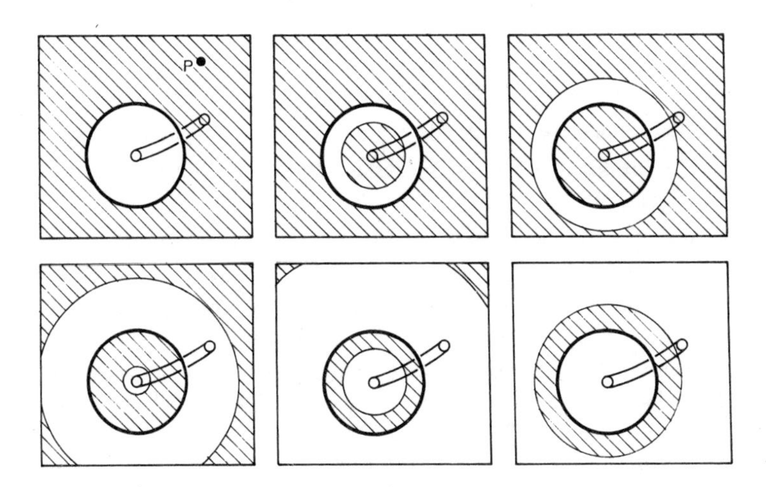

Fig. 18. An undermined distinction, and successive stages in the outward propagation of a value and its re-entry through the tunnel.

changing from 'marked' to 'unmarked' or vice versa as it crosses the boundary, and re-entering through the tunnel. The value at any fixed point P would then flip between 'marked' and 'unmarked' continually as if a train of square waves were passing it.

This introduction of time permits the use of the calculus in the design of switching circuits, and the main text ends with a diagram of an arrangement that flips from one value to the other every second time a variable within it flips; i.e. it is a counting device, and it has practical applications, being 'the first use, in a switching circuit, of imaginary Boolean values in the course of the construction of a real answer'. Finally, in two appendices Spencer-Brown uses his calculus to prove the axioms of Boolean logic, and gives it an interpretation by identifying the marked state with 'true' and the blank space or unmarked state with 'false'.

This extraordinary construction (epoch-making, indeed, if it accomplishes what it claims to have done) was written in a style of Pascalian grace, if not with irreproachable clarity; its air of stark rigour contrasted strangely with the somewhat shamanistic view of the mathematician it implied, as the one who brought back almost incommunicable truths from a distant and dangerous Otherworld:

> To any person prepared to enter with respect into the realm of his great and universal ignorance, the secrets of being will eventually unfold, and they will do so in a measure according to his freedom from natural and indoctrinated shame in his respect of their revelation.
>
> To arrive at the simplest truth ... requires *years of contemplation*. Not activity. Not reasoning. Not calculating. Not busy behaviour of any kind.... Simply *bearing in mind* what it is one needs to know. And yet those with the courage to tread this path to real discovery are not only offered practically no guidance on how to do so, they are actively discouraged and have to set about it in secret, pretending meanwhile to be

engaged in the frantic diversions and to conform with the deadening personal opinions which are being continually thrust upon them. In these circumstances the discoveries that any person is able to undertake represent the places where, in the face of induced psychosis, he has, by his own faltering and unaided efforts, returned to sanity. Painfully, and even dangerously, maybe. But nonetheless returned, however furtively.

What appealed to my temperament most deeply in *Laws of Form* was its conceptual knife-play. 'The theme of this book is that a universe comes into existence when a space is severed or taken apart,' says Spencer-Brown in an introductory note. As a beginning, this move has its precedent: 'The earth was without form, and void.... and God said, Let there be light: and there was light ... and God divided the light from the darkness.' That the basis of existence is difference, that the first step in understanding is discrimination, is for me an axiom that feels as if it were innate. As it happened, while I was dealing with Spencer-Brown's diagrams I was also writing a catalogue note for an exhibition of abstract paintings by my closest friend, Peter Joseph, and I borrowed Spencer-Brown's dictum as an epigraph:

'... a universe comes into being when a space is severed ...'
... a world in which the divisions of night from day, the shores, the horizons, are sharp enough to cut you. In the paintings of '67-8 Peter Joseph reduces landscape to the clearest oppositions of the simplest elements, each work being composed of just three or four rectangles of pure colour.... One of these paintings, a long rectangle divided once from top to bottom and once from side to side to give four identical areas, conveys the sensations one would hope for from a trans-polar orbiting: three of its quadrants, in brilliant but somehow sombre primaries, have an arctic, auroral, chill; the fourth contains six months of night.

What is gained by such a severe process of reduction? In these condensed transcriptions of experience, all ambiguities of twilight, poetry of misty horizons, flux and riddle of coast-lines, are suppressed in favour of the immediacy of the great elements. One comes out of a cave, and faces the sky; one crosses the brow of a hill, and there is the Atlantic....

I sent a draft of this to Spencer-Brown, looking for permission to quote from his then unpublished book, and later phoned him. He sounded mildly interested in my poetic application of his words, and I arranged to call on him at his flat in Richmond. I found him to be a middle-aged man with a dark and intellectually hungry look, a shadow of D.H. Lawrence projected into abstract realms. He was very ready to expound his discoveries, though a little short with my mathematical ignorance; as a student, his IQ had been 'off the clock', he told me. He scribbled in the flyleaf of my proof copy of *Laws of Form* a little diagram of how *i* is re-entered into its defining equation, as mentioned above. He identified his 'marked and unmarked states' with the Yang and Yin of Taoism – concepts I had thought long worn away to nothing by mindless overapplication. But his counting device, a stack of circuits like the one described above that counts to two, each feeding its output into the next, and so registering a number in the binary system, was a very concrete application of his theories; it was patented, he told me, and used in the real world by British Rail for keeping track of the number of railway wagons entering and leaving tunnels. Spencer-Brown had developed this device in collaboration with his brother, whom he mentioned also as the discoverer of some abstruse equations for which he 'had to go very far'. The impression I came away with of this brother was slightly mysterious; he seemed to combine an uncanny degree of intelligence with a certain mythical remoteness from the actual, like Holmes's Mycroft.

Mathematics cohabited with mysticism in Spencer-Brown's

bookshelves. I noticed J.W. Dunne's *An Experiment With Time*, which had caused a commotion in the 1920s by purporting to make precognitive dreams scientifically respectable. Dunne argues that since time passes, there must be another time with which to measure how fast it passes, and yet another to measure the passing of that, and so on; also, we have a consciousness, a consciousness of that consciousness, etc., corresponding to this infinite number of time-dimensions, and that these higher-dimensional consciousnesses are (naturally!) able to see at least some way into the future of ordinary everyday time. H.G. Wells had been impressed by Dunne at first but later said his thesis was 'an entertaining paradox expanded into a humourless obsession'. I had early learned to sneer at it, but now Spencer-Brown put me right; Dunne had grasped the importance of 'recursion' (the sort of snake-swallowing-its-own-tail process exemplified by Spencer-Brown's expressions that re-enter themselves), and had merely lacked the mathematics to develop it.

Peter Joseph's exhibition was due to open at the Lisson Gallery soon thereafter, and I invited Spencer-Brown to the opening. M and I arrived a little late, and found him looking rather adrift among the gallery-going crowd. We stayed him with conversation. I asked – it was out of order as party chitchat, but I did want to know, having been fiddling with the question inconclusively – if his arithmetic of indications was isomorphic with the arithmetic of the null set and the universal set. ('Isomorphic' is jargon for 'structurally identical'.) He concentrated inwardly for a few seconds before answering, 'Yes.' He seemed a little put out, so I hastened to add, 'I suppose no one ever thought to write down the arithmetic of the null set and the universal set.' 'Quite!' he replied. Later an exotic girl, prime ornament of the art-gallery set of that season, black with a bloom of gold-dust, came in, and we all turned to admire her. M said she could see purple smoke rising from her, and Spencer-Brown explained that that was because she was seeing her directly; if the light-level had been lower the girl's 'essential body' would have been visible hovering above her head.

During one or other of my two encounters with Spencer-Brown we talked of the four-colour hypothesis, which was then still unproven. This is one of the most famous problems in mathematics, quite simple to state but doggedly resistant to solution. It arose as follows. In 1852 a Francis Guthrie, colouring a map of the counties of England, found that he needed only four colours to avoid having adjoining counties (i.e. counties sharing a length of border, not just a point) of the same colour. Would this be the case for any map, however complicated? he asked himself, and being unable to answer the question he put it to William De Morgan, his former mathematics teacher at University College London. De Morgan immediately passed it on to his colleague Alexander Hamilton in Dublin. Neither of them could prove that four colours are always sufficient, nor disprove it by concocting a map for which they are insufficient. Later the American logician, Charles Peirce, and Arthur Cayley, Professor of Mathematics at Cambridge, tried and failed with it. In 1879 Cayley's former student Alfred Kempe published what was thought to be a proof of the hypothesis, and became Sir Arthur Kempe FRS partly on the strength of it. But its strength was not sufficient; in 1890 P.J. Heawood, a lecturer at Durham, found a subtle mistake in Kempe's reasoning. Much more penetrating but very laborious techniques were invented to attack the problem as an understanding of its difficulties deepened over the next eighty years. It was realized that a proof might depend on consideration of a number of special configurations of map-regions, the obstacle being that this number was dauntingly large and some of the configurations intractably extensive. Such was the state of play at the time I was occupied with *Laws of Form*.

In this book Spencer-Brown had claimed that his use of imaginary values would lead to the proof of certain unspecified theorems beyond the powers of a mathematics based only on real values; in fact, he wrote, 'I may say that I believe that at least one such theorem will shortly be decided by the methods outlined in the text. In other words, I believe that I have reduced their decision to a technical problem which is well within the capacity of an ordinary mathematician who is prepared, and who has the patronage or other means, to undertake the labour.' This theorem, he now told me, was to be the four-colour theorem. Furthermore, he had an idea that its solution was deeply connected with one of the most famous outstanding problems of the theory of numbers, Goldbach's conjecture, that any even number bigger than 2 can be represented as the sum of two prime numbers (for example, 36 = 31 + 5) – a simple statement that has no known exceptions, having been tested for numbers up into the quadrillions, but that has not yet been proved to be true of all numbers however vast. I was intrigued by this coming dragon-hunt: would my strange acquaintance march out, armed with imaginary values, and triumph on the shadowy horizon of the known?

In the following years, having moved to Aran, I did not keep in contact with Spencer-Brown and heard no more of him. Then in 1976 came an announcement that left the mathematical world both dumbfounded and disappointed. Two mathematicians, Kenneth Appel and Wolfgang Haken of the University of Illinois, claimed to have proved the four-colour theorem, having got the number of special configurations down to about 1500 and carried out elaborate calculations on each. But as well as their own ingenuity and skill their proof had called for 1200 hours of computer time. Few seriously doubted that they were right, that the theorem was true – but could one call this a proof, if the nub of it was miles of computer print-out that no human could ever check, and, more fundamentally, if it provided no insight into *why* the result was true?

A few months later a friend sent me a newspaper cutting of an interview with Spencer-Brown, described as a maverick Cambridge mathematician. The announcement of Appel and Haken's proof had spurred him on to produce a proper, readily comprehensible, proof using his own methods, which involved thinking 'in a way that almost blows the mind'. It took him, he said, just two weeks; then he thought that if there was one proof there must be another, and proved it again by a different route. He was to present his proof in a lecture, and leave his diagrams and tapes of the lecture with London University.

It was strange to me that I never heard another word about this proof. Books I picked up now and then on contemporary mathematics retold the saga of the computer proof, but Spencer-Brown was unmentioned. Was he an exploded myth, a forgotten eccentric? However, when I began to explore the Internet in the late '90s I discovered the existence of a Spencer-Brown cult. It was also clear that much highly professional work was being done in the field established by him, even if the accounts of some of it emanated from institutions with unreassuring names. From Jack Engstrom of the Maharishi University of Management I learned that:

Louis H. Kauffman ... has applied *Laws of Form* to topology, natural numbers, electronic circuits, imaginary values in logic, and other areas. Francisco Varela extended *Laws of Form* into biology, autopoiesis, three-valued logic, and cognitive systems. William Bricken has used it for logical calculations on computers and has applied it to natural numbers. Jeffrey James has applied it to real and imaginary numbers. I have applied it to natural numbers, to set theory, to a philosophy of transcendence, and to a philosophy of wholes and parts. Nathaniel Hellerstein has applied *Laws of Form* to a logic of paradox. *Laws of Form* has also been applied to neural processing, automata, semiotics, and more.

Eventually I tracked down an Internet mailing list entitled 'Spencer-Brown in America', to which other searchers as puzzled as myself had posted notices. One of them read:

Dear list members; Now I wonder whether anybody knows anything about Spencer Brown. The more autopoietic systems theory I read, the more central does the concept of form seem to be, which allegedly origins from Spencer Brown. Spencer Brown himself, however, seems to be both a key- and a shadow-figure at the same time. What is Spencer Brown up to at the time being? For some time I assumed him dead. Wrongly, it seems....

An eminent Princeton mathematician, John Conway (known to followers of the theory of artificial intelligence as the inventor of 'The Game of Life') had replied to such queries:

In his 'Laws of Form' he recasts some of logic in a very elegant new way, but it can't really be said that this removes the paradoxes from formal logic. I don't believe his 'proof' of the 4-color theorem (and don't know any other professional mathematician who does). When he first made this claim, I bet him 10 pounds that his proof wasn't valid. At that time, it wasn't written down, but he spent a good few hours describing it. I told him that I certainly wasn't going to pay up without having seen a written copy of the proof, and I'm still waiting to do so!

I posted a query myself to this mailing list, calling it 'À la recherche de Spencer-Brown', and over a year later my query was answered by a journalist who had entertained Spencer-Brown in California. His headlong e-mails brought to my desk a slipstream of excitement off the western world's leading-edge of innovation:

tim i saw your message about g. spencer-brown, via john conway, dated 3 jan1998, only recently on the internet; you can find much information about spencer-brown at the laws of form web pages, http://user.aol.com/lawsofform/lof.html.... perhaps you've found him by now. a couple of people are currently working on applications of laws of form: dick shoup of interval research in palo alto (shoup@interval.com) and william bricken (bricken@halcyon.com). shoup is developing logic systems that calculate using imaginary values. eventually he wants to build field-programmable gate arrays that can be programmed on the fly, in microseconds, so that a chip can be a graphics accelerator on one cycle and a cpu on another. he thinks this is essential for when silicon hits the wall and moore's law works no more. shoup's systems are written in a laws of form computer language called losp, which is a variant of lisp written by bricken.... i'm sure either he or shoup would be glad to help you out – email them and mention that i gave you their addresses. they're great folks. (interval, you may know, is paul allen's private think tank in palo alto.) as for the four-color theorem, you may have seen spencer-brown's letter to nature in 1976 in which he announced that he had a solution. it was just after the publication of this letter that brown came to california for a couple of months, a riotous experience. i introduced him to some people who hired him to lecture at xerox parc on his proof, and apparently it was a disaster – no one could follow it.... i did visit your website and was fascinated by the maps. i thought your illustrations for laws of form were just perfect....
all the best, cliff barney

Gratified to learn that my humble hackwork was appreciated in this world of great folks with private think-tanks, I dashed to the 'LoF web site', and found a cornucopia of curious references. A *Vita* of our hero suggested a personality driven by the imperative of excelling in every field. For instance, in the Royal Navy he qualified as a Radio Mechanic with the highest mark of all candidates in the practical examination, and later undertook successful trials of hypnosis for dentistry and the rehabilitation of wounded personnel; at Cambridge he captained the University chess team when it beat Oxford, qualified without dual instruction for the Silver C Badge in gliding in the world-record time of 78 days, joined the Cambridge University Air Squadron and became the first *ab initio* member of any university squadron to qualify for Instrument Rating, led the Formation Aerobatic Team to victory in the Cambridge Squadrons Formation Flying Contest, learned racing driving with Gavin Maxwell, worked with Wittgenstein on the Foundations of Philosophy and appeared with the University Actors in a Shakespearean production. As a professional psychotherapist he used hypnosis and sleep-learning techniques to enhance performance in sporting and other competitive activities, and specialized in the education of superintelligent children. As adviser to the Federal Naval Research Laboratory in Washington, DC, he made discoveries in optics, coding and code-breaking. He has worked with Lord Cherwell on Goldbach's conjecture and with Bertrand Russell on the Foundations of Mathematics, been Soccer Correspondent to the *Daily Express* and Bridge Correspondent to *Parson's Pleasure.* Apart from some Visiting Professorships he has worked mainly as an engineer, and he runs his own publishing house. His recreations are as various as his professional activities; they range from shooting to Mozart, from writing and singing ballads to constructing ingenious machines and inventing games.

Laws of Form, I learned from the LoF site, had evolved from edition to edition, and in 1994:

a fourth preface was added in which he talks about 'triunions' or 'triple identities' such as of reality, appearance and awareness, or imaginability, possibility and actuality, or what a thing is, what it isn't and the boundary between them. He claims/acknowledges that Sakyamuni (the Buddha) is 'the only other author who evidently discovered these laws.' He invites the reader to join a siblinghood and help found a school of his methods for intuitively feeling and naturally acting upon the consequences of there being nothing. He ... asks for money and volunteers to help him found schools for superintelligent children such as he was.

The consequences of there being nothing! This took me back to a passage from which I had averted my attention in *Laws of Form*:

There is a tendency, especially today, to regard existence as the source of reality, and thus as a central concept. But as soon as it is formally examined, existence is seen to be highly peripheral and, as such, especially corrupt (in the formal sense) and vulnerable.... It is the intellectual block which most of us come up against at the points where, to experience the world clearly, we must abandon existence to truth, truth to indication, indication to form, and form to void, that has so long held up the development of logic and its mathematics.

That the world has produced itself out of nothing, I do believe, utter mystery though it be, and that we can trace the self-creation of its elements back to the very seedgrain of time – but there falls the cliff edge, the ultimate distinction; was Spencer-Brown sacrificing the existent to the formal structures of its possibility? This did not suit the naïve-realist side of my temperament, my sense of the clamorous demand of every blade of grass on the clifftop for recognition. I began to find references to him on the Internet and elsewhere that were disquieting in other ways too. In the *Scientific American* of February 1980 Martin Gardner had disparaged Spencer-Brown in his well-known column 'Mathematical Games':

In December of 1976 G. Spencer-Brown, the maverick British mathematician, startled his colleagues by announcing he had a proof of the four-color theorem that did not require computer checking. Spencer-Brown's supreme confidence and his reputation as a mathematician brought him an invitation to give a seminar on his proof at Stanford University. At the end of three months all the experts who attended the seminar agreed that the proof's logic was laced with holes. But Spencer-Brown returned to England still sure of its validity. The 'proof' has not yet been published. Spencer-Brown is the author of a curious little book called *Laws of Form*, which is essentially a reconstruction of the propositional calculus by means of an eccentric notation. The book, which the British mathematician John Horton Conway once described as beautifully written but 'content-free', has a large circle of counter-cultural devotees.

In the mouth of Gardner (whom the anarchic philosopher of science Paul Feyerabend has called 'the pit-bull of scientism'), 'counter-cultural' would be a term with bite. What had urged him to this attack? To my amazement I found a letter of Gardner's, of slightly earlier date, quoted on two web sites including the Math Forum discussion group, saying that he had proposed to write a column on Spencer-Brown but had been dissuaded by another mathematician, Donald Knuth, on the grounds that to do so would give publicity to a charlatan! What could this work be, that seemed to have provoked a move to suppress it? Although I had little confidence in my ability to judge it, I was determined to look into it.

The only available account by Spencer-Brown of his controversial proof of the four-colour theorem, I gathered from the LoF site, was in an English appendix to a German edition of *Laws of Form*, to be had from a company called Astro. When I located Astro's website I was discouraged to find it largely concerned with astrology and sexual magic. In any case, they failed to respond to my e-mails, and so, with some trepidation (one Internet source having described him as 'a dreadful curmudgeon but at the same time one of the most charming, humorous, and delightful people I have ever met'), I wrote to the author himself. I was hoping for some closure to the story of high intellectual endeavour I wanted to tell and of which I had already written the earlier part; it would have been satisfying to see the new proof victorious over all doubters, so that the conclusion of my essay could carry it in procession as Cimabue's new Madonna was carried by the admiring townsfolk of Florence. Instead, I have become, briefly, the Fool of pelting storms, too fraught with personal matters to be recounted here, far out on a conceptual heath. How simple it would be to round off this adventure if Spencer-Brown and his proof were, 'not in lone splendour hung aloft the night', but glittering away up there as unquestionable constellations with Pascal and his mystic hexagram! But I have discovered, with pain, that the realm of pure ideas is one of the battlefields of human affairs, of which we will never have a colourable map.

A week or so after the date of my letter, the telephone rang: George Spencer-Brown himself, from his new address in the West Country. He began with a long complaint that the telephone number on my letterheading did not include the international dialling code, continued with some disobliging remarks on a little book I had sent him on prime numbers by a friend of mine, and half an hour later he was still telling me about his own astounding discoveries in the theory of prime numbers, including an unpublished proof of Goldbach's conjecture. I arranged to send him a cheque for the price of the German edition of *Laws of Form*, which arrived a few days later together with a photocopy of a long and rather bizarre-looking handwritten paper on prime numbers, and a twenty-page letter in which he dealt at length with the dialling-code question again, again abused my friend's book, went into a rant against G.H. Hardy and *his* book, ('a [mediocre] mathematician's apology [for being mediocre]'), broke off to include a poem 'In Praise of Lying' by Richard de Vere, presumably a pseudonym of Spencer-Brown himself, got into his stride by remarking that if he is let loose in any mathematical discipline, he will either abolish it or transform it, and ended with a rich account of his dealings with God, Sir Stanley Unwin and Bertrand Russell over the publication of *Laws of Form*.

Several parts of this inordinate communication infuriated me, and I wrote a riposte calculated to raise blisters on a battleship, but did not put it in the post because at the same time I was reading the new work on the four-colour theorem and finding it full of wonders. Instead, I devised a challenge, in a logical format that recurs in Spencer-Brown's own writing:

Dear George – It was generous of you to send the ms on primes between squares with the copy of *Gesetze der Form*. I'm nibbling my way through it slowly line by line with pleasure and excitement, as I am the four-colour proof. I hope shortly to be able to write something about my wonderment over the pure silk of your mathematics, even if I fail to follow the threads all the way to the conclusions.

However there were several passages in your letter that angered me. I have written a sharp retort but refrained from posting it. What to do? I propose that you choose whether to receive my expression of wonderment, or my retort, or both, or neither. If you choose not to choose, I will choose which if any to send you. But I think you should choose. Yours sincerely …

His reply completely ignored this provocation; without even a preliminary 'Dear Tim' it opened with the claim that the only two great mathematicians of the twentieth century were

Ramanujan and himself, and that while Ramanujan was probably the cleverer I would already know that Spencer-Brown was the deeper. What was I to make of this? If false, the boast was absurd; if true, then it is to be expected that he would know it to be so, and it would be legitimate, if unconventional, to proclaim it. The question added to the interest of the journey I made to visit him, as a gesture of friendship and concern, in the summer of 2000.

I found Spencer-Brown to be a vigorous seventy-odd-year-old, with the fine domed head one associates with the conventional image of genius, and combative bushy eyebrows. He is still extremely productive – the floor of his cottage was ankle-deep in calculations – but in cramped circumstances, having held no academic post since the early 1980s when he was Visiting Professor of Mathematics at the University of Maryland, because, he claims, of the sort of calumny I had come across on the Internet. He has been denied outlet for his papers other than as appendices to successive editions of *Laws of Form* – a shame, this, because it is a classic text, and in its current form suffers as a Palladian villa would from disproportionate extensions and ad hoc lean-to sheds. His conversation was challenging (we disagreed on the fundamental nature of reality, because, he said, I was 'unenlightened' – which remark enlightened me instantly to the fact that Buddhism can be as oppressive as any other system of belief), amusing ('Most cats think the way to play chess is to knock the pieces off the board and chase them around the floor; but my kitten, having spent up to two hours sitting on my shoulder while I analyze a chess position, knows how to put out its paw and gently push a bishop from one square to another'), sometimes profound ('To write a great book one must love one's reader'), but unremittingly self-centred, so that after a few hours my own ego was struggling for oxygen.

When I picked up the phone to call a taxi, I found that the spiral flex between handset and base was so intricately twisted that I could only prise them a few inches apart, which made speaking difficult. During our subsequent telephone conversations I have often thought of that flex, for they have been extremely tangled and contorted. Calls would go on for an hour or more, leaving me sometimes with a valuable insight into Spencer-Brown's mathematics and sometimes with a burden of history, too personal in relation to himself and libellous in relation to his fellow professionals ('pipsqueaks', the most of them) to be anything other than an obstacle to my writing of this account, and on several occasions ending in as much physical violence as can be transmitted by telephone.

He had some unfair advantages, I felt, in these bouts: an extraordinarily quick intelligence; an unshakeable belief in the correctness of whatever he was saying, even if, or especially if, it was the exact opposite of what he had said last time; and an utter ruthlessness as to my *amour-propre*. Sometimes I tried to hang up on him, but he was always quicker on the draw and while I was still aiming a parthian shot I would hear the decisive click of his receiver. Latterly I undertook such exchanges with the enthusiasm I might have for running before the bulls of Pamplona, in expectation of an exhilarating scamper ending with a high probability of being trampled and gored. The relationship terminated, as M had predicted, with my dismissal into the category of pipsqueak. I had written asking for elucidation of certain steps that left me doubtful in two of his proofs of the four-colour theorem; there was no reply, and I accepted the break in this overheating correspondence with some relief, but eventually, since I needed guidance in order to progress with the mathematics, I telephoned him.

A useful little tutorial followed, but when I showed a reluctance to follow him in a death-defying leap from a result in *Laws of Form* to the obvious truth of the four-colour theorem he told me that if I couldn't see the connection, after the thousands of poundsworth of free tuition he'd given me, I was an idiot. Like all the mathematicians who couldn't or wouldn't read his work, I just wasn't good enough. And he rang off. I rang back instantly to remind him that despite his rudeness I would be writing about him, and was finally annihilated by another roar of 'You're not good enough!'

So, the message of all that sound and fury is: *Caveat lector*; any idiocies in the following sketch of Spencer-Brown's reformulation of the theory of maps are my own. In any case I can hardly go beyond the opening moves here, but I hope to convey something of the finesse of his approach. I begin by quoting the introduction to his own presentation:

> Once I had constructed the primary arithmetic in *Laws of Form*, I became aware that I had a technique that, suitably applied, would solve the map-colouring problem. I did not immediately apply it to the problem, because I felt that to make what would almost certainly be a difficult proof, in a completely novel system of mathematics, would occasion the hostility and disbelief of the more superficial members of the mathematical profession.... This subsequently turned out to be the case.
>
> In 1961 my brother came to visit me and I showed him the problem. He went away contemptuously, saying,
>
> 'Soon prove *that*!'
>
> After a week he returned with the news that it was turning out to be more difficult than he had at first anticipated. But he had found an astonishing algebraic colouring algorithm [i.e. a rule-bound procedure for colouring any given map] ... In 1975 my father died, leaving an estate worth half-a-million pounds (a substantial sum in those days) that had been in the family for more than two centuries. My mother who, for vindictive reasons, maintained that my brother and I 'did not deserve it',

forged documents and, with the connivance of her lawyers, succeeded in stealing it all and bequeathing it to my cousins, leaving my brother and me destitute. The unpleasantness and the distress of it killed my brother and nearly killed me.

It was in these circumstances of despair and bereavement that I decided things could not get worse, so I might as well prove the four-colour theorem. My brother's algorithm was now lost, so I set about it the only way I knew how, using two elementary marks to set up the special case.

A map, of the abstract sort we are considering, consists of a number of regions separated by borders, drawn on a flat surface; we count the area one would normally think of as outside the map (as the sea is outside a map of Ireland) as one of its regions. The points where borders meet are called nodes. Adjacent regions are those that share a border (not just a node). The shapes and sizes of the regions and borders are irrelevant; we can stretch and bend them as convenient. The first step is to standardize the map so that just three borders meet at any one node, as in Fig. 19. If the four-colour theorem is true for standard maps it must be true for all maps; so from here on we need only consider standard maps.

Suppose we have a map that can be coloured (so that no two adjacent regions are of the same colour – and from now on we will take this clause to be understood) with just four different colours. An economizing printer looking at this as a production problem might hit on the idea of using a red and a blue ink, say, plus a pur-

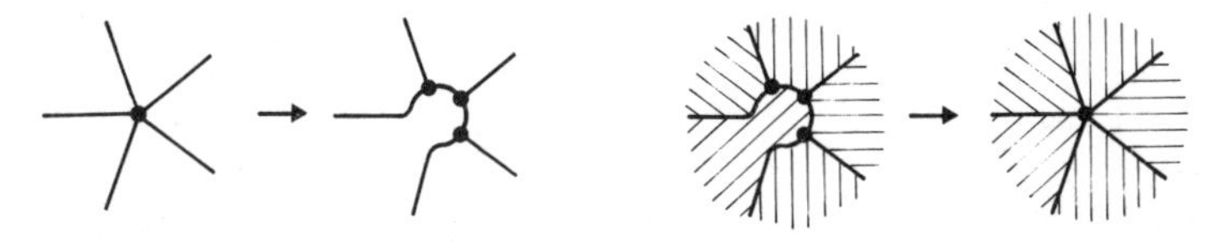

Fig. 19. *Left*: Eliminating a node at which more than three regions meet by expanding one of them. *Right*: If the map containing this new configuration can be four-coloured, so can an otherwise identical map containing the old configuration.

ple made by overprinting red with blue (or vice versa), leaving the white paper to represent the fourth colour; this is the format: *r*, or *b*, or both, or neither. Thus the four-coloured map could be printed from two plates, one of a number of red shapes and the other of a number of blue shapes – i.e. the map can be *factored* into two nodeless maps each of two colours (red and white, or blue and white), rather as the composite number 15 can be factored into the prime numbers 3 and 5 (Fig. 20). Spencer-Brown's strategy is to prove that *any* standard map can be so factored – from which it follows that any map can be coloured with just four colours.

Without going too far into the lengthy reasoning necessary to capture this proof, I can give the willing reader a glimpse of the striking techniques for manipulating the colourings of maps that Spencer-Brown has devised on the basis of the above simple ideas. First we shift attention from the regions of the map to its network of borders. Fig. 21 shows how the borders of the four-coloured map shown in Fig. 20 are made up from the borders of its two factors. Note that at each node borders of three types meet. We can think of them as having three different colours. A little experimentation will convince the reader of the theorem (first published by P.G. Tait in 1880) that if a map can be four-coloured, its net-

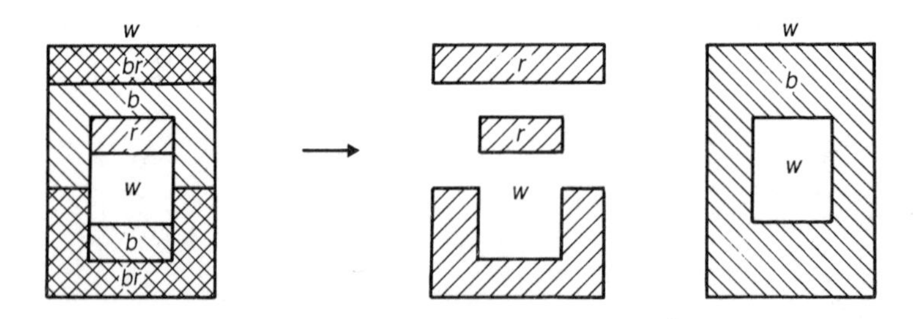

Fig. 20. A four-coloured map and its two-coloured factors.

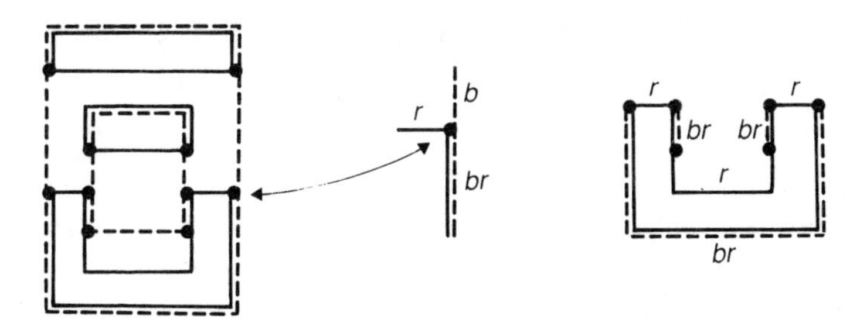

Fig. 21. The three types of border in a four-coloured map, and the alternation of types of borders around one of its regions.

work of borders can be three-coloured (i.e. coloured so that the three borders meeting at a node are all of different colours), and vice-versa. So the problem of four-colouring maps has been reduced to one of three-colouring (standard) networks. Just to show that this is a real problem, here are two little labyrinths, in one of which lurks the beast, uncolourability (Fig. 22). By trial and error the ingenious reader will be able to colour the first, but the other, a fascinating entity known as the petersen, cannot be three-coloured; in fact it is the smallest of all the uncolourable

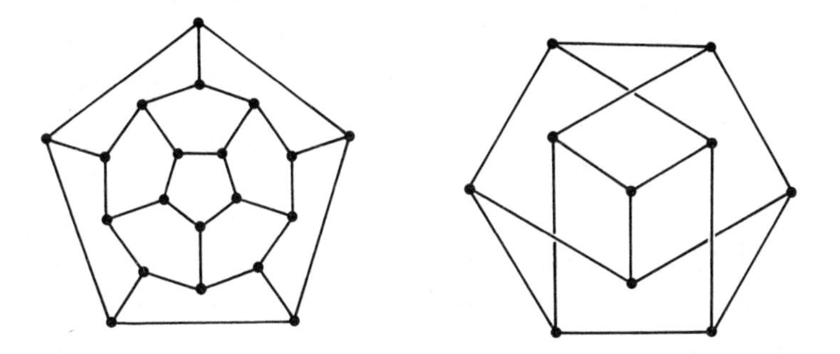

Fig. 22. A symmetrical map (derived from a regular solid, the dodecahedron), colourable with some puzzling, and the petersen, an uncolourable network.

networks. It is three-dimensional, and since its links pass under and over each other they cannot be the borders of regions in a map; so it is not a counter-example to the four-colour map theorem. (One of Spencer-Brown's proofs of the theorem proceeds by showing that all uncolourable networks must be three-dimensional, from which it would follow that all planar networks are colourable.) It is instructive to try colouring the petersen, starting from any node and working outwards, labelling the links 1, 2 or 3, adhering to the rule that the three links meeting at any node must have different labels. Whatever choices one makes in this process, one soon finds oneself trapped in a corner where one cannot avoid breaking the rule. The sensation is like that of coming up against a contradiction in a chain of reasoning, or of trying to work out whether the statement 'This statement is false' is true or false. Paradoxicity, not uncolourability, is the relevant paradigm in this mathematical situation, according to Spencer-Brown; the network *is* colourable – but only with imaginary colours analogous to the imaginary values he introduces as solutions of self-contradictory equations in *Laws of Form*. (This is the great leap from *Laws of Form* to the four-colour theorem that I jibbed at, in that last apocalyptic telephone conversation.)

I shall try to convey the fascination and simplicity of Spencer-Brown's methods and follow him some way into the theory of map colourations. Returning to Fig. 21, we can take the three colours of the network to be blue, red, and blue-red, i.e. purple (*b*, *r*, and *br*). Of course at this stage we do not know if all maps can be four-coloured, or, equivalently, if all planar networks can be three-coloured; so we have to be able to represent a link we cannot colour or which we choose to leave uncoloured. Fortunately we have the fourth alternative in Spencer-Brown's logical

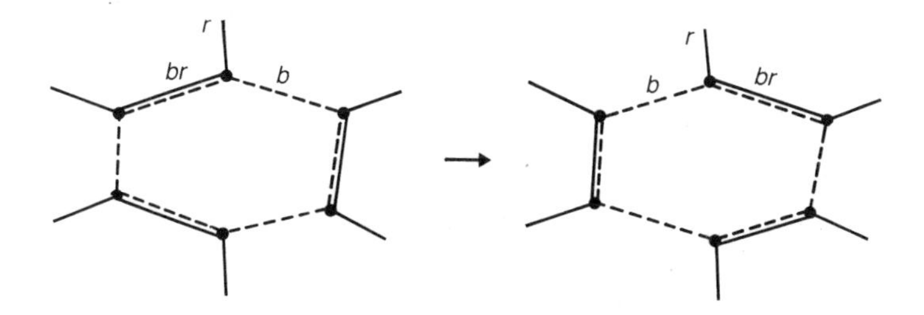

Fig. 23. Interchanging the two types of border round a circuit.

pattern, neither *b* nor *r*, for such a link. Note that the links involving *r*, for instance, form closed circuits, around which they alternate: *r*, *br*, *r*, *br* etc. (These circuits are just the boundaries of the colour-patches in the *r*-factor of the map.) Suppose we have succeeded in three-colouring a network in which there is a circuit as shown in Fig. 23. Clearly we can interchange the *b*-links with the *br*-links without having to change any of the *r*-links and so upsetting the colouration of the rest of the map. This is the sort of operation one often needs to perform in map-theory, and Spencer-Brown has invented a brilliant way of thinking about it. Imagine one could take a closed band of colour *r* and superimpose it on the circuit. What are the rules for superimposing one colour on another? (Instead of 'superimpose' we should say 'idempose', as the two colours will not just be one on top of the other but will occupy the identical space.) The answer goes to the heart of what Spencer-Brown calls 'formal mathematics', that is, the mathematics of elements whose order, size and shape are undefined or irrelevant. Consider a region in a map, and another region of the same colour idemposed on the map so that part of its border coincides with part of the border of the first region (Fig. 24). Since we have the same colour on either side of it, we can omit the doubled part

Fig. 24. Eliminating borders between two regions of the same colour. (For clarity the two borders are shown slightly separated where they in fact coincide.)

of the border; the two regions fuse like raindrops, eliminating the surface films between them. This suggests that the rule should be that idemposition of two identical elements cancels both of them:

$$rr = \quad .$$

(Of course real colours do not behave in this way; we have to idealize them somewhat in order to use them in the representation of abstract, formal, elements.) This 'Axiom of Idemposition' relates profoundly to *Laws of Form*. Fig. 24 is analogous to one of the primitive equations of the arithmetic of indications,

$$\overline{\quad}| \; \overline{\quad}| = \overline{\quad}| \; ,$$

and if one of the regions totally surrounds the other the two borders cancel each other completely, which gives us the other primitive equation,

$$\overline{\overline{\quad}|}| = \quad .$$

It follows that if we idempose a band of colour r on a circuit made up of alternating links b, br, b, br, etc., all the b-links will become br-links and all the br-links will become b-links, since $brr = b$. This is exactly the operation shown in Fig. 23.

I will take this exposition just one step further. A typical situation in network-colouration arises when all the links have been

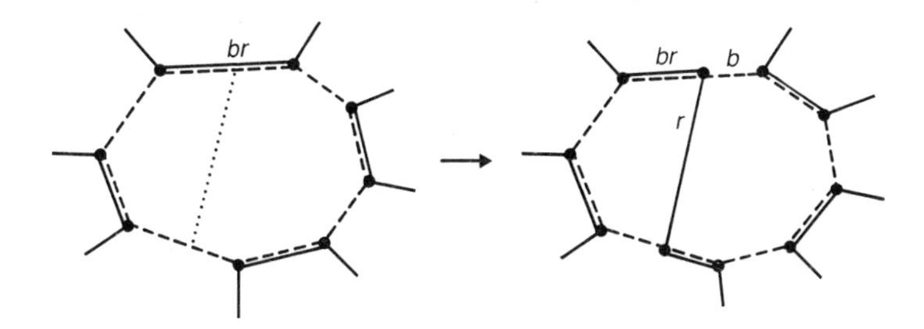

Fig. 25. How to colour a link spanning a circuit.

coloured except one. Suppose the uncoloured link spans a circuit of alternating *b*-links and *br*-links, as in Fig. 25. As things stand we cannot colour it in correctly because there would then be nodes at either end of it in which two identically coloured links meet. But if we run an *r*-band around the closed path made by the uncoloured link and either the left-hand or the right-hand half of the original circuit, all is well; the missing link is now coloured *r*, and the links joining it at top and bottom are *b* and *br* . Since none of the links connecting this circuit to the rest of the network have been changed, we have coloured in the last link without upsetting the rest of the colouration.

Beyond this point matters become increasingly complicated. A series of theorems is deduced, rich in content and succinct in expression, whcih seem to me much more vivid than the tedious demonstrations standard texts on the subject drag one through, only to abandon one in the Sahara Desert of the computer proof. But perhaps I have said enough to persuade the reader that Spencer-Brown provides the tools with which the four-colour theorem can be broached. In fact he claims that

> ... if the four-colour theorem were false ... the whole of *Laws of Form*

would be invalid. But since *Laws of Form* clearly is valid, the four-color theorem must be true. This is so evident, even without further elaboration, that it was considered an adequate proof of the color theorem by all the major mathematicians to whom I published it in the early 1960s, Bertrand Russell, JCP Miller and DJ Spencer-Brown.

As for the proof published by Haken and Appel in 1977, according to Spencer-Brown:

It may, or may not, be possible to prove the color theorem the way they claim. What is now certain is that they did not do so.... Of course they did not set out with the dishonest intention of claiming a proof they did not have. No one but a fool would do that. They must have felt certain that what remained to be done would be easy, and that they could do it between the announcement and the publication. And when they found it wasn't and they couldn't, there was no way to save face except to brazen it out.... You might have thought, somewhere in that mass of obscurely written jargon there might be a proof lurking. I am afraid you will be disappointed.... It is the most ridiculous case of 'The King's New Clothes' that has ever disgraced the history of mathematics; the imaginary 'proof' has been pumped out with propaganda and millions of dollars of misguided public money, and none of those involved now dares admit that nothing of any value has resulted.

And the obverse of this canonization of the Haken-Appel proof has been, he tells me, the demonization of Spencer-Brown. His own proofs have only appeared in rather obscure quarters, and few mathematicians have troubled to learn enough of his techniques to appreciate them; no 'experts' followed the seminar Martin Gardner referred to. I myself have spent many days with his papers, and can report that not only are they without taint of charlatanry but they contain mathematics of Mozartian grace and clarity. Once the extremely compact symbolism has been unpacked, most of the concepts and methods are of luminous simplicity. Spencer-Brown has great faith in the mathematical ability of youngsters (he writes somewhere to this effect: 'If a child asked me for a toy I would say, "Here is the number system. It costs nothing, it will give you entertainment for a lifetime – and you can't break it!"'), and I can envisage future generations of school children enjoying the way his operations send colour-changes flickering all around networks and suddenly reveal the way to colour in that last link.

But do these innovative methods lead to unshakeable proofs? The four-colour theorem is notoriously a logical Bermuda Triangle into which many a bold flight of intellect has vanished. A difficulty in coming to a judgement here, apart from the complexity and subtlety of his arguments, is Spencer-Brown's persuasion that certain quite complex mathematical facts are obvious and hardly need demonstration. For instance one of his proofs follows, he claims, from a certain 'self-evident proposition' – and he then interjects, 'If you do not yet see this as self-evident, do not persist with this proof.' Of the four-colour theorem itself he writes, 'Everybody knew it was true, so it must always have been subliminally obvious. And this is what made it so difficult to prove.... Subliminal awareness goes to the heart of the problem, but consciousness invariably takes a long way round before trying anything simple.' The mathematician, through repeated mental handling of abstract objects, acquires a feel for their properties which is as difficult to convey in explicit terms as our sense of the leverage and balance of knives and forks. Whether such surehandedness can be delusory, whether in the particular case of Spencer-Brown's grasp on the four-colour theorem there is no slippage and fumbling, is beyond me to say. But, if pressed – and the momentum of this essay does press me – I would risk a claim that once some clarifications have been carried out, gaps made good, and the smoke and dust of a paradigm-shift have settled, his proof will appear in all its originality and irrefutability. And of this I am sure: an injustice has been done him, and a body of mathematics that should have been subjected to the normal trials by peer-criticism has been disregarded. That is a crime against both truth and beauty – for Keats's equation of those two excellencies holds better in mathematics than in any other field.

THE ECHOSPHERE

Searching the London Library for old books that might throw light on the history of Connemara, I came across *The Saxon in Ireland, or, the rambles of an Englishman in search of a settlement in the west of Ireland*, published by John Murray in 1851; anonymous, but with the name John Henry Ashworth written into the title page by librarian's pencil. Its professed intention was 'to direct the attention of persons looking out either for investments or for new settlements, to the vast capabilities of the Sister Island', and it goes into great detail on the manuring of land, the Incumbered Estates Act, and other practicalities; I suspect it was also intended to boost the author's own courage and that of his family in facing emigration to the Ireland of that still famine-stricken date, for it is remarkably positive in outlook, and one has to read the small print of quoted matter in the appendices to find a mention of potato blight. I did glean a few grains of information on Connemara, but it was an incident from his travels in Mayo that has lodged in my mind. In Ballycroy, a remote glen of Erris, the author calls upon another Englishman, Mr S, who tells him about the strange meeting which led to his own settling there. This episode, quite out of keeping with the rest of the book, is entitled 'The Echo Hunter'. I have trimmed it a little.

I was at Ballina, sitting at the open window of the inn, when the melodious sounds of a bugle, playing a beautiful Irish air, attracted my attention. No long time had elapsed when a little dapper-looking gentleman, of middle age, entered the room, with a bugle in his hand. 'I have to thank you, sir, I presume,' said I, rising and bowing, 'for the great treat I have just enjoyed?' 'You have to thank me for very little, sir,' replied he, carelessly; 'This instrument is all very well, but I seldom use it except to rouse Dame Nature, whom you will find sleeping among the crags and cliffs. The moment I sound my bugle, an answer comes from the mountains, no less singular than beautiful, leaping from rock to rock, now loud, now murmuring, but always sweet.'

'Excuse my dullness,' said I, smiling; 'I understand you now; you mean the echo.' 'Why yes,' he replied, 'echoes according to the common language of the world; I call them the voice of awakened Nature. There is nothing in the theory of sound that can satisfactorily account to me for the wonderful voices my bugle has awakened in certain spots which I have discovered; but I do not make them generally known, for – laugh if you will – I have a notion, which I like to encourage, that Nature loves solitude, and would ill brook the being disturbed by every common idler. I have travelled through and through Ireland, meeting with such echoes in many a sequestered nook, unnoticed by any one before me, but Ballycroy, yes, sir, not twelve miles from hence – Ballycroy exceeds them all. But,' said he, lowering his voice, 'it were vain for you or any other mortal to attempt to find out these peculiar spots. I alone discovered them, and with me the knowledge of their existence will die.'

Ere we parted for the night, he invited me to accompany him on the following morning on an excursion into the Ballycroy mountains. He placed me on a certain spot; and exacting a promise that I would not follow him, he retired, and in about a quarter of an hour gave me such a treat in his peculiar art as I can never forget. The rocks and mountains seemed alive with harmony; the softest and wildest notes floated in the air, now close, now distant; now dying away in some distant recess of the valley, now awakening louder and louder among the cliffs and precipices;

at one moment faint as the whisper of the breeze, at another loud, clear, and bold as the trumpet of the Archangel. I never before or since experienced the sensations which at that time overpowered me, and I no longer either smiled or wondered at the zeal of my new acquaintance in his peculiar and eccentric pursuit.

Ballycroy was at that time for sale. Mr S was moved to buy it up, and subsequently turned the wilderness into a valuable property. Only once after that did he meet the Echo Hunter:

When I last caught sight of him, he was leaning pensively against the rock, round whose base we turn on entering the glen below us. He congratulated me upon my improvements, but declared significantly that 'Art would drive out Nature.' 'This', he said, 'is my last visit to this valley; it was once a favourite spot of mine, but the presence of man has tainted it. In Corranabinna I am safe from intrusion. There man will never pitch his tent; it is too near the sky.' After we had parted about ten minutes, a few discordant notes of his bugle awakened a thousand more discordant echoes, and I never saw him more!

'The Saxon' is both affected and encouraged by Mr S's story, and when it is finished the two of them sit in silence for some time. Looking out on the comfortable scene of 'pastoral wealth' Mr S has created, he feels a strong conviction of his own success in a similar experiment. That the discord, quite obviously, is between the profits of cultivation and nature's loss, is not spelled out, and the book goes on its way as if the Echo Hunter had never sounded such a note.

Since those days in which a new dispensation of capitalism was replacing the old landlords bankrupted by the Famine, development of Ireland's 'waste lands' has advanced, very slowly and with many setbacks. The land had to be drained of tears; one cannot forget that, in weighing up profit and loss. Also, areas such as those I have been concerned with in the western counties have not been untouched wildernesses for several thousand years; humankind has settled them intensively in some periods, building, cultivating, naming. In fact this is the sort of land I love, that has been finely and repeatedly discriminated into multitudinous place by use of stone and word. I have peeped into the Grand Canyon and rapped on the windows of a Norwegian glacier, but such life-threatening giant terrains are not central to the map of my empathies. In the west of Ireland are territories where a proportion is still preserved; nature has room for its ways and so does humanity. This sphere of interaction and qualified autonomies has its echoes and the echo hunters necessary to their awakening, its sheerest cliffs have names and histories, its placelore knows a gradation of familiarity from town centre to lonely upland. Without defining it more tightly, I'll call it the Echosphere; the word has been lying around in my mind for years awaiting an application.

Descending to the local and personal scale of my time in the west of Ireland, which has coincided with a surge of economic growth, I am as aware of cultural loss, loss of history, loss of echo, as I am of ecological damage. I have come to resent the truth-telling of environmentalism; a sense of the Earth's vulnerability and of the obligation to defend it hangs a veil of anxiety between me and the landscape. At every turn of my walks I expect to find some detail of the scene that I have lovingly and scrupulously noted in one of my maps or books, effaced by careless 'improvement': a JCB levelling a site for a house has needlessly scooped away an old limekiln; a road-widening scheme has heaped rubble onto a stone commemorating the death of a friar at the hands of priest-hunters. Is it mere ignorance and indifference, or does some wordless animosity drive this destruction of the countryside and the little landmarks that make it meaningful?

In 1998 I was asked to write a background note on Connemara for the programme of the Druid Theatre's first production of Martin McDonagh's plays *The Beauty Queen of Leenane*, *A Skull in Connemara*, and *The Lonesome West*. I took it as an opportunity to release my pent-up rage in a diatribe directed against all that I had previously written on Connemara:

A CONNEMARA IN THE SKULL

We don't see much of the outside world in McDonagh's trilogy – a cemetery by night and a favourite lakeside suicide spot are the only excursions allowed from his comfortless kitchens. In the first play we hear: 'All you have to do is look out your window to see Ireland. And it's soon bored you'd be. "There goes a calf."' Is the Connemara out there a fit setting for these desperate comedies? If so, it is not the Connemara of cloud-shadow connoisseurs.

This crossbones landscape is the outcome of six thousand years of human demand. Stone Age agriculturists fired and felled the oakwoods; already by the Bronze Age peat bogs were spreading across exhausted soils. Centuries of bog growth almost closed off the interior and confined history to the shoreline. The potato came, and an exploding population crammed into a narrow coastal zone was forced to strip the peat away, as fuel for itself and for the growing city of Galway, leaving naked granite. When the potato rotted, in 1845-49, a frugal and ingenious peasant ecology, already screwed to the limit by an extortionate social system, collapsed into beggary and despair. Connemara still lives in the aftermath of millennial famine, of age-old physical and psychic deprivation. Who were the expropriators? Is it true, as one of McDonagh's characters holds, that the 'crux of the matter' is 'the English stealing our language, and our land, and our God-knows-what'? For the record – and it is complex and ambiguous – the masters of Connemara from the Middle Ages to the

Cromwellian victory in 1650 were the Gaelic O'Flahertys, and folklore associates every one of their castles with murderous tyranny. In the Leenane area the Joyces, originally Norman-Welsh but thoroughly Irishized, held power under the O'Flahertys and later adapted profitably to the role of middlemen under the new landlord instated by the post-Cromwellian settlements, Trinity College Dublin. The will to exploitation is general; the opportunity for it passes from hand to hand.

When, towards the end of the last century, agrarian terrorism forced the British government to undertake the development of the West, one result was that the landlords were bought out, the companionable old clusters of hovels broken up, and the former tenants installed in isolation, each family in its own cottage on its own stripe of land. Was this one of the traumas, along with the death of the Irish language and the sealing up of the oral tradition, that has made rural life an insult to its setting in nature and the past? A walk in today's pastoral landscape is a succession of affronts to one's sense of belonging in the world. Stroll up the boreen: you may remember it as charming from ten years ago, but you will find that the flowery hedgerows have been ripped out in favour of barbed wire, and that the old cottage is roofless, replaced by a gaunt bungalow facing a huge shed of concrete blocks and galvanized sheeting. In the slovenly yard is a silent dog condemned to life on the end of a chain. Cross a hillside black from the burning-off of furze, all its larks' nests, lizards and butterflies incinerated; skirt round the dead sheep caught in briars by its neglected tangles of wool; stride out with relief across the open mountainside. But the heathery slope has been turned into an irreparable morass by overgrazing, the ruthless grant-driven multiplication of undernourished ewes too weak to feed their lambs. If you meet the shepherd of this desert of suffering, he will tell you he must be compensated before he considers reducing his flocks so as not to leave his own children a barren inheritance. There is more, much more. The news from Connemara's waters is equally squalid:

brown-trout lakes contaminated with sewage, slurry and fertilizers, the salmon's spawning beds overwhelmed by peat washed down from the eroding mountain, sea trout with their fins eaten away by lice from the concentration fishfarms in the bays …

No need, I hope, for me to say that this is not the only Connemara – I have written at length about beautiful and hopeful Connemaras – but there is no doubt that this Connemara exists, this calamitous backdrop to the society McDonagh shows us, fled by its young, with its brutalized law and its old church gone in the teeth. The machine of his theatre forces us to laugh even as we pity and shudder at all this, and the bare beauty of Connemara is one of his grim implicit jokes. Perhaps it is even close to the 'crux of the matter'.

However, in case after case, there is no time for correct philosophical naming of the crux of the matter; something is under immediate threat, and action is called for. I will note some phases of two campaigns I have been conscripted into by obligations incurred through writing.

★

Roundstone Bog is a terrain I became aware of through the writings of the naturalist Robert Lloyd Praeger even before I came to live in Roundstone itself; indeed it was one of the factors behind our settling here in 1984. A mere half-hour's walk from the house, it lies far outside the habitual; it offers extremes, physically and mentally. I can best introduce this aspect of it through a piece I wrote for the launch of *Nature in Ireland*, John Wilson Foster's study of Irish natural-history writing, in 1998:

TWO WET DAYS IN ROUNDSTONE BOG

Recently a few dozen members of the British Ecological Society visited Connemara, and I joined them one very wet morning for an expedition into Roundstone Bog.

All horizons had been dissolved by rain. Middle distances were grey on grey; lakes lay like deflated clouds on the blurry levels. But underfoot everything was intensely individuated by colour and pattern, as if the scientists' acute attention were highlighting each plant's characteristic features. The behaviour of water too was remarkably various once one had come to terms with the general wetness; it spilled in a rippling film over grass like combed hair, flowed in lacework channels around heathery tussocks, stood feet deep with pondweeds stretching up through it. In one pool were skinny growths of a particular sedge, like arrows frozen in the act of darting out from the margins as if to possess the water surface (and the ecologists confirmed that this was a stage in the transformation of a pond into a dry hummock). Every plant had its role in the self-creation of the bog. We scattered, leaping from tussock to tussock, splashing through shallows, balancing precariously across quaking beds of sodden vegetation. When someone, bent over a specimen, called out in puzzlement, wonder or triumph, we clustered again for discussion.

And then we came across something that gave us pause. On top of a hump of sphagnum lay a spreading or dropping or splashing of something yellow – the vividest yellow one could visualize, an artificial-chemical, mustard-gas-warning yellow. The stuff covered an irregular area a few inches across; it stuck up in flaccid peaks like stale custard. We gathered round and looked at it; I was the only one who ventured to poke at it with a finger. It was crusted, resilient. 'A slime mould', one of the experts decided, and added, 'No one knows much about slime moulds, not even whether they're plants or animals. In the textbooks they come somewhere between the fungi and the algae.' And we left it at that.

I have since looked up slime moulds. They have a complex lifecycle. A spore germinates and produces a few cells, of what sort depends on circumstances. In a suitably moist environment they are amoeboid and equipped with whip-like organs of motion; in drought they become cysts, armoured for endurance, waiting to revert to the soft and mobile when times improve. These 'swarm cells' pair by fusion, multiply by hundreds of thousands to form a mass of protoplasm, not divided by cell walls but with its nuclei scattered throughout it. In some species this 'plasmodium' is brightly coloured or white, in others colourless. It can ingest particles of vegetable matter – hence the possibility of classifying it as an animal – and will migrate if food runs low. Finally it sprouts 'fruiting bodies' from which spore will be released. The only life-stage one is likely to come across casually is the plasmodium, the sluggish handful of naked protoplasm in search of what it may devour.

'Slime', according to Sartre, 'is the agony of water.' This cryptic formulation occurs near the end of his Being and Nothingness, *as he is working his way towards its climactic summation: 'Man is a useless passion.' 'The slimy', he says, is one of those material qualities felt to have a moral dimension, as revelations of potential relationships between conscious beings (the 'for-itself', in his terminology) and the inanimate (the 'in-itself'). Whereas liquidity connotes the self-enfolding, elusive, flow of consciousness, and hardness the obstinate otherness of the in-itself, the slimy is an ambiguous, treacherous, in-between mode of being. It can be picked up, but then it cannot be relinquished; it clings, stains, corrupts. Its ultimate threat is of engulfment, losing oneself to the inert, being overwhelmed by one's materiality. As such it is 'antivalue' itself, all that is to be shunned and skirted around in one's appropriation of the world, in the human project of becoming God (which, God being a contradiction and an impossibility, is, as he says, 'a useless passion').*

This slime mould out on Roundstone bog, this blob of protoplasm 'tout entière à sa proie attachée', is Life at its most alien, repulsive, and fascinating. Are we, humankind, part of this? Is it part, or indeed all, of us? Does it represent our individual mortality, our generic potential immortality? Let me worm my way into this complex of responses to Nature through an account of another wet day in Roundstone Bog.

This day, some sixty years ago, was the occasion of a most remarkable meeting of minds. Praeger describes what he calls the 'quaint scene':

> *A number of botanists had forgathered for a kind of symposium on bogs, held in the middle of one of the wettest of them. We stood in a ring in that shelterless expanse while discussion raged on the application of the terms soligenous, topogenous and ombrogenous; the rain and wind, like the discussion, waxed in intensity, and under the unusual superincumbent weight, whether of mere flesh and bone or of intellect, the floating surface of the bog slowly sank until we were all half-way up to our knees in water.*

Praeger's anecdote, from The Way that I Went, *is an attractive family snapshot of science renewing itself from generation to generation; for among those present were Knud Jessen, the Danish pioneer in the reconstruction of long-ago floras from pollen grains preserved in bogs; Arthur Tansley of Oxford, the first writer on bogs as ecological units; Praeger himself, botany's most human face in Ireland; and a then very young Frank Mitchell, who also recalls that day in his* The Way that I Followed. *But there is something more to our reception of this story. A nihilistic or anarchic part of us wants the scene to be continued, the assembled mighty intellects to go on sinking, until nothing is to be seen on the surface of the lonesome wetland but a few bubbles, still uttering those long words: soligenous – pop! ombrogenous – pop! What is going on in this fantasy? Mind is being reabsorbed into matter; humanity's imposition of language, order, meaning, is being sucked down and choked off by Nature. As we well know, some future environmental Armageddon could lead to a world without mind. And that vanishing is a possibility we are not entirely reluctant to entertain, because of our guilt in the face of Nature. The joyous unproblematic stride with which Praeger traversed his forty botanical subdivisions of the country (a scientific equivalent of the revivalists' literary, linguistic and mystical reappropriations of Ireland) is not for us; everywhere we are brought up short, for instance by the moral and physical squalor of modern farming which has reduced many of his beloved western hillsides to black mud and barbed wire. Nor can we wholeheartedly join in his delight in the 'feeling of being akin to nature – of belonging here, just like the living creatures and the living water'. Life, understood without transcendental escape-clauses, is a tangle of dire implications. Ecology, the science of oneness-with-Nature, has acquired a spuriously benevolent tone but is not all balance, sharing, tolerance and harmony, for parasitism, territoriality, population crashes and mass extinctions are all good ecology; 'animal rights' are to life, liberty and the pursuit of prey.*

However, perhaps the opposite scenario will be enacted, that is, of Nature entirely absorbed into mind. As our knowledge of Roundstone Bog piles up in thesis after thesis, the thing in itself disappears. Overgrazing, turfcutting, forestry, draining, fencing; and on the other hand, Rural Environment Protection Schemes, Special Areas of Conservation, National Heritage Areas, Environmental Impact Statements: intensive and extensive ordering of the wild and the wet by bureaucracy. In centuries to come perhaps only a few last sods of turf will be preserved, in the form of holograms. By then humanity, if it could still be so called, will be existing without Nature, almost without reality. Our consciousnesses will have been amalgamated, compressed and downloaded onto the galactic internet. Every atomic particle will ultimately be pressed into service for our databank, until there is nothing in the universe but information. We will then not merely 'know the mind of God', as Stephen Hawking puts it, but will have reconstituted the Cosmos as mind; we will be the mind of God.

A melancholy prospect. One could imagine such a mind pulling the plug on itself, flickering out, saying to reality: Goodbye, better luck next time.

The material world either purged of mind by ecological catastrophe, or reduced to a hallucination by technological progress – these are two forms of universalized insanity, apocalyptic exaggerations of the dismal alternatives that face us in actuality if we don't change course, change ethos, reduce our numbers, reduce our environmental footprints, etc. Whatever its outcome, we are presently living on the cusp of this history. An unheard-of rate of destruction of the natural world is twinned with an unprecedented effort to record it. So, as a happy side-effect, ours is a golden age of natural historiography; and whether the gold is of sunrise or sunset we can't tell. Nowadays there is so much worthwhile publication in the field that we might think there is more nature around than formerly. One reason for this, as John Wilson Foster ironically notes, is 'our increasingly modest redefinition of what constitutes nature'. Another factor is the power of the instruments, both technical and conceptual, that we train upon the ever dwindling object. So, for example, 92 per cent of our bogs are gone, and we have John Feehan and Grace O'Donoghue's magnificent production, *The Bogs of Ireland*, to sharpen our sense of loss. But Foster's *Nature in Ireland* is not at all despairing. I read in it this quote from René Dubos:

> Ecosystems possess several mechanisms for self-healing … they undergo adaptive changes of a creative nature that transcend the mere correction of damage; the ultimate result is then the activation of certain potentialities of the ecosystem that had not been expressed before the disturbance.

If that is so, and if the process of readjustment does not involve removing us, the originators of the disturbance, then the proliferation of fine nature-books can be seen as potentialities of the ecosystem we inhabit. If indeed we can bring our regretful new awarenesses to bear in assisting this *transformation, we will not need to become God in order to prevent Nature doing away with us. In that case our wonderful new natural histories will be our readmission tickets to Paradise.*

⋆

So Roundstone Bog is for me an occasion, a locus, of wild speculation. It is, as they say, 'far out'. But when it comes to defending it against the great wrecking-machine of commerce, such values have to be kept hidden; the State is not likely to declare it a Place of Philosophical Importance. One has to join battle on what for me are uncongenial grounds: small print of European and national legislation on the environment; bureaucracy of governmental and non-governmental bodies concerned with conservation; calculations of the tourism market and the economic worth of landscape.

In 1981 a large proportion of Roundstone Bog was designated as an Area of Scientific Importance (ASI), and while the designation in itself had no legal effect the County Council took note of it in their County Plan, making it difficult to obtain planning permissions for developments within it. In 1987 scientists from the Wildlife Service redrew the boundaries of the ASI, extending it a mile or so north-westwards towards Clifden, the little town that thinks of itself as the capital of Connemara. A year's delay then ensued, during which the updated maps of the ASI lay in the Office of Public Works and no one, not even the Galway County Council, was informed of the change. By mischance it was during this interregnum that a group of Clifden hoteliers decided that Connemara's tourist industry needed an airport and that the ideal site for it would be on the part of the bog nearest to Clifden, in a townland called Ardagh which, so far as anyone not privy to the OPW's in-tray knew, was not part of the ASI. Their plans were quite ambitious: a three-quarter-mile strip that could take planes as large as the Fokker 50; upgrading of an almost untraceable old bridlepath across the bog into an approach road; a terminal building tastefully thatched to placate the environmentalists. A number of local businesspeople were seduced by this image of an up-to-the-minute Connemara, and put money into the scheme.

All looked hopeful for them until the boundary change came to light and it appeared likely that permission would not be granted. A furious row broke out in the local press; property values were being affected by faceless bureaucrats who could arrive out of the blue and draw a red line around your land that prevented you profiting from it, without even informing you of the fact. The Clifden Airport Group launched an energetic campaign against such oppressions, drawing on the support of farmers who were incensed to discover that they were no longer eligible for grant aid towards the afforestation of their 'waste land' if it lay in an ASI. Eventually the question went to the High Court and the ASI procedure was found to be unconstitutional – quite rightly, from the point of view of commonsense and justice, but at some cost to the environment throughout Ireland, which is still awaiting the implementation of the revised scheme of designations, the 'Special Areas of Conservation'. The outcome in Connemara – largely the fault of the OPW – has been an anti-environmentalist backlash, which is only now fading as another thoroughly commercial reality makes itself felt; the tourist's liking for unspoiled scenery.

At the height of the dispute Leo Hallissey, a schoolteacher in north Connemara who also runs annual courses for adults on the environment, asked me to participate in a series of public meetings with the aim of explaining to the public why Roundstone Bog was worth conserving. (To those who had scraped a laborious living off it by sheep-rearing, and who were just discovering the financial delights of forestry and machine turf-cutting, this was by no means obvious.) Hastily Leo and I, and a few people we could count on for effectual support in the neighbourhood, named ourselves as 'Save Roundstone Bog' (which, we explained, in a phrase that became wearisome to me, was 'an ad hoc group of concerned residents'). SRB's first public meeting, in Roundstone, was fairly well received; the Roundstone people had not been much infected by the Clifden enthusiasm for aeronautics, which they rightly suspected would benefit principally a few hotels in Clifden itself and the golf course nearby. But our second meeting, boldly staged in a hotel lounge in Clifden itself, was eventful; in fact I found it most disturbing and exciting. The Clifden business interest was there *en masse* – in fact 'mass' was the impression given by their bulky black overcoats filling the back of the rather cramped and overcrowded room. After three or four brief talks (on the wildlife of the Bog, on its scenic values and the artists it had attracted, and – my echospheric contribution – on its placenames and folklore), there was a general discussion which rapidly became extremely contentious. A populist Connemara politician with whom I had had one or two previous disputes over environmental matters worked himself up into a fury over a letter to the *Irish Times* from David Bellamy, the respected conservationist, eccentric presenter of TV wildlife programmes and eminent Professor of Botany, whom we had canvassed for his support in this controversy. Professor Bellamy had written, tactlessly enough, that

> Yes, the tourist potential of the key areas of the Irish heritage must be opened up, but it must be done in a totally environmentally friendly way. To even consider siting an airport, or any other development, within the Roundstone Bog catchment area is an act of pure stupidity and vandalism.

Here we have, roared the politician, brandishing the newspaper, someone with an address in London saying that Connemara men are vandals! – and he continued with such rage against this Englishman, as he insisted on calling him, that one of the Airport Group's more physicalist supporters suddenly leaped out of their ranks at me with fist clenched, roaring, 'And here's another … Englishman we should throw out!' Fortunately he was some distance from me and his impetus spent itself on empty air. For a while there was uproar. I was shocked, and at the same time exhilarated. Obviously the interruption could only be to our advantage. I stalked up and down with a long face while Leo, who was in the Chair, tried to quell a shouting match. Then I solemnly demanded silence, emphasized that something extraordinary had just occurred and that such a remark had never been made to me in all my twenty years of living and working in the west of Ireland, and I called on the meeting to repudiate it. Our supporters in the audience all rallied round with paeans of praise for my contributions to Irish culture; there was a formal motion condemning the intervention, which the opposition party had to support; and we returned home the moral victors.

Victory on earth proved more elusive. The dispute has lasted more than a dozen years now and has gone through many phases it would be tedious to detail. Every stage has demanded the writing of innumerable letters and e-mails, the calling of meetings, circulating of petitions, soliciting of expert opinion, raising of funds. The Airport Group organized a plebiscite in west Connemara and doorstepped house to house; we held aloof from it, knowing we would lose handsomely and relying on the claim that this was not a question to be settled by local headcount. Here I am in the middle of their campaign, responding to a hostile columnist in the local paper, the *Connacht Tribune*, in which most of the verbal battles have been fought:

THE BATTLE OF ROUNDSTONE BOG

These are madding times in Connemara. Even as I write I hear a loudspeaker car drumming up attendance for a pro-airport meeting with a cheerful song that sounds from here as if it were trying to rhyme Connemara with banana. My Apple Mac is red hot from drafting appeals, rebutting criticisms, sharpening shafts, even trying its hand at ballads on the Roundstone Bogodrome. I enjoy the cut and thrust of the debate; sometimes I cut deeper than I'd intended, and regret being carried away by my indignation at some slur on a colleague which is difficult to counter without disproportionate, detailed, fuss. But below this superficial excitement there is sadness and weariness and disgust.

Disgust, for instance, at the bleating of meaningless slogans ('People First! Vote for Progress!'). Disgust at the whiff from attitudes and misconceptions that I had thought dead for decades ('Let the environmentalists come to Connemara on donkeys since that's the sort of society they want to preserve!'). My weariness is induced by the endless re-use of arguments that have been demolished a dozen times in print. These come up in abbreviated form nowadays, like 'It's only a bit of old bog!' – as if there were no distinctions to be noted between upland bog and the rarer oceanic lowland blanket bog, between bog that has been ruined by machine turf cutting and bog that is still miraculously intact, and above all between all other bogs and Roundstone Bog itself, which has no parallels anywhere on the Earth! Or this other argument, the jewel in the intellectual crown of the airport lobby: 'All we want is thirteen acres! Aren't the People of Connemara worth thirteen acres of bog?' This is the area to be taken up by runway, access roads, etc., and of course it is very small and is being used to imply that negligible damage will be done by the project. However, runways and roads are essentially linear features and their area is not the important factor. After all, a cut is something of negligible area, but can be lethal. The other half of the argument, invoking the People of Connemara, is of course standard demagogic tactics, discounting the views of all those people of Connemara and elsewhere who happen not to agree, and ignoring commonsense doubts about whether an airport really would have enough effect on unemployment in the long term to justify irreparable damage to the beautiful scenery on Clifden's doorstep. However, we shall hear the argument again, I prophecy, and again and again and again.

But sadness is the most abiding emotion I feel about this dispute, for many reasons, private and public. A well-argued article (with the conclusions of which I disagree) in the Connacht Tribune *of a fortnight ago tells me that 'Tim Robinson appears to have misread the airstrip situation entirely. It must be painfully obvious to him that his opposition to the airstrip is not widely appreciated and contrary to what the majority of Connemara people want for their community.' Well, I am not a pollster or a politician, I don't arrive at my opinion by reading the public mood or estimating which way the majority will swing. If a writer has a function in the community it is to try and think things out for himself or herself, and not just in a tiny local and short-term context either. It is indeed painful to be embroiled in a dispute with some of the inhabitants of the place I have made my home in, but I have only once been abused as an Englishman – and even that incident, which shocked me at the time, was, I am told, no worse than many an altercation in the Council chamber ...*

To see what really matters about the project, what the landscape really is, other than a source of money, walk out of Clifden across the old Ard-

bear bridge as generations of local people and visitors have done, and look at the view from the little hill of Dúinín. Immediately below is a little stream flowing into and out of a small lake, by which is a picturesque patch of old woodland. On the far side of the stream, in the bog, is a strange rectangular boulder of rough marble, where the famous Father Myles Prendergast used to celebrate Mass in secret, in the years of oppression that followed the defeat of the French-led rebellion in 1798; he was a participant in that tragedy and afterwards escaped from prison to live as an outlaw in Connemara for several decades. This rock, then, is the foundation stone of the Clifden congregation, of which he is listed as the first parish priest. Beyond that the bog spreads wide, golden or purple or grey according to the seasons, flowing up and over a low rise into a labyrinth of streams with a hundred lakes, as far as Errisbeg Hill, which arches its back like an angry cat against the southern sky. Such sights are good for the soul! Clifden holds something in trust here for the human spirit, for ever. And just here, between the lake and that first low ridge, is where they want to put in three-quarters of a mile of concrete runway, access roads, a terminal building, high wire fencing and parking for a hundred cars. Please, do not let them do it.

★

Despite a satisfactory result for the Clifden Airport Group in the plebiscite, some years then passed in which the project seemed to have been abandoned, most people having come to the conclusion that in economic terms it was a fantasy. Then in 1998 the sleeping dog woke. The Group was now looking at another site, on the western margins of the Bog, which for historical reasons happened to belong to the State. Wearily I once more rounded up the faithful ad hoc and alerted the national environmentalist organizations:

ANOTHER THREAT TO ROUNDSTONE BOG

The tranquillity of Roundstone Bog, probably the finest stretch of lowland blanket bog still left relatively undamaged, is threatened once again by a proposed Clifden Airport. The Clifden Airport Group, a private company, now wants to put a 600-metre strip on the bog in Derrygimlagh by the remains of the Marconi Telegraph Station (disused since 1922), which belongs to the State. The Minister for Arts, Heritage, Gaeltacht and the Islands, Ms. Síle de Valera, and the Minister of State Éamon Ó Cuív, are considering leasing part of the Marconi site for this purpose to the Clifden Airport Group.

Save Roundstone Bog, an ad-hoc group of local residents and others concerned to protect the environment, are actively opposing the project. Bord Fáilte, The Heritage Council, An Taisce, BirdWatch Ireland, Irish Wildlife Trust, Irish Peatlands Conservation Council, Earthwatch, and Voice of Irish Concern for the Environment, as well as PlantLife and the Conservation Council in London, have all expressed their concern. Eminent wildlife experts who oppose the scheme include Prof. Victor Westhoff, Prof. David Bellamy and Éamon de Buitléar. A large number of individual objections have gone in from Connemara and elsewhere, including several from local hoteliers, business people and farmers.

The Marconi site itself is not included in the proposed Special Area of Conservation which will give most of Roundstone Bog some protection, but it immediately adjoins it and is an integral part of the whole bog complex, only separated from the rest by a narrow lake, Loch Fada. Because it is so close to the heart of Roundstone Bog, any development here would intrude on the silent beauty of this unique tract of wilderness and compromise its status as a wildlife habitat.... Even a small strip could be the thin end of the wedge. Once the ban on construction is breached, there is no knowing what might be allowed in the future: a flying club? a holiday village? Job creation is important, but developments that damage Con-

nemara's most attractive features to the visitor, its spaciousness and peace, are not the way to go about it.

★

Our submission to the Minister, who had called for observations on a proposal to exchange part of the Marconi site for the 80 acres of bog owned by the Airport Group at Ardagh, had to be more carefully argued. The tone was measured, sober:

Dear Minister
We would like to thank you for ensuring that a range of opinion is consulted before the proposed exchange is considered.... In our explorations of this issue we have found concern on four levels: for the general tranquillity and freedom from aircraft noise of Connemara as a whole; for the ecological and aesthetic integrity of Roundstone Bog; for the future of the Marconi site itself; and for the independence in planning matters of the National Parks and Wildlife department. A summary of the arguments on each count is appended.

We present this document as responsible inhabitants of Connemara, unmotivated by commercial considerations or political affiliations, and concerned for the natural world as well as the local community. We trust that it will be read, and we hope, acted upon, in the same spirit of commitment to the general good....

... and so on, with inexorable urbanity, the four levels of concern sprouting into twelve numbered arguments, the document presenting itself as iron logic in the velvet glove of courtesy.

The outcome of this second round in the Battle of Roundstone Bog appears to have been successful. The Minister of State announced that a search would be undertaken for an alternative site for the airstrip (a project he favoured in general because of the potential link to strips on the offshore islands of Inishbofin, Inishturk and Clare Island), and that a conservation plan would be drawn up for Roundstone Bog. This alternative site, with which he hoped to disarm both sides in the controversy, was soon located, in a less sensitive locality near the Clifden–Cleggan road. While I did not believe that an airstrip even of the small size now envisaged was necessary or desirable for Connemara as a whole, there were arguments in favour of the links to the islands. I felt that the pros and cons had been reduced to local significance and that the argument should now be left in the hands of those immediately advantaged or disadvantaged by the scheme. Personally I was ready to accept the new proposals as a compromise, being mindful that ongoing controversy itself is an interruption to the wellbeing of the community. Save Roundstone Bog has evaporated in a sigh of relief, and there is even a springtime of reconciliation in the air; one of the chiefs of the Airport Group has told me that I should be proud of what I had achieved for Roundstone Bog. I would qualify that by noting that no permanent institution has emerged from the campaign, to research, educate about and protect the Bog, which will always be under threat.

However it has acquired one defence it lacked before, and that is, an identity. Local people remark on the fact that visitors now enquire for it and seek it out. Until recently those thousands of acres of rocky hummocks, quaking bog, lakes and streams had no name as a whole, being regarded only as so much waste land subject to various turbary, grazing and shooting rights defined in terms of about twenty townlands and parts of townlands. Praeger, the first writer to call attention to its uniqueness within the British

Isles (in *The Way That I Went*, 1937), could refer to it only as 'the great bogland behind Urrisbeg', from Errisbeg Hill which rises out of its southern margins. So a name has long been necessary for the whole ecological unit, and somehow that of Roundstone Bog has been adopted, whereas it could as well have been Clifden Bog. While I do not think that I invented this name I cannot find any earlier written uses of it than a 1987 essay of mine in which I said that 'at least the core of this area, which is becoming known as Roundstone Bog, having been spared by forestry and commercial turf-cutting so far, should most certainly be preserved as it is; apart from its ecological uniqueness, it harbours one of the rarest of resources, solitude'. What ignorance of conservation realities that phrase 'at least the core of' reveals! I soon moved on to a realization that the whole, together with its margins, must be conserved, for if we let the margins go then the next layer in becomes marginal and will be lost in the same way. When I published my map of Connemara in 1990 I took care to stretch the label 'Roundstone Bog' over the entire tract from edge to edge. It is the ultimate privilege of the cartographer, or topographical writer, occasionally to create a place out of nowhere.

⋆

I was very happy that the airport controversy had come to an end, not only because of the repeated interruptions to my own work it had caused, but because I resent the label 'environmentalist' that naturally attaches to me after so many published words on such themes; I fear it obscures a proper literary reception of my books. Going deeper, I feel a distressing tension between what I call 'true writing' and the opportunistic, rhetorical mode one can insensibly fall into in polemics. Never, in real writing, would I use a cliché like 'the thin end of the wedge' – but what a dense, sharp, formulation it is, what a handy tomahawk in a scalping raid! As for the pillaging of my books and essays for juicy phrases and memorable images to be recycled in press releases and letters to newspapers, that is in absolute contrast to my usual care not to repeat myself, for my rule is, when I find that I am falling into repetition, to take it as a challenge to rethink, to invent the unsaid. There are good reasons for the writer, the artist in any mode, not to use the skills that have been acquired in the practise of it to advance arguments in support of any already defined position however meritorious. True writing, art in general, is essentially concerned with what is yet to be defined, what may become defined through its exercise but then is to be left behind in the advance into the unknown. But if the ivory tower itself is on fire, such arguments go up in smoke! And then the best one can do is to accept the plunge into campaigning as a temporary reincarnation as salesperson or politician, which can be educative for the reality-starved introvert.

However, writing itself incurs obligations to its subject. Perhaps if I had not written that essay on Roundstone Bog I might have left it to others to fight for it when the time came. When in 1999 I heard that planning permission was being sought by Inis Meáin Co-op for three 150-foot-high wind turbines on the south shore of the island, in a landscape to which I have devoted countless words, I tried to ignore the fact, until it rankled so much I had to attend to it and inform myself of the details. The Aran Islands had been recently connected by submarine cable to the mainland electricity grid, and the scheme was to sell electricity to the ESB as well as to power a desalination plant. When it became clear that no one else was going to initiate opposition, I began the all-too-foreseeable procedures once again. First I called the wildlife writer Michael Viney about it; he thought that I was 'on a hiding to nothing', given the environmentally correct connotations of wind power, but undertook to raise the subject in his weekly *Irish Times* essay. This gave me a peg to hang a letter to the paper on:

Michael Viney's column of 12th June mentioned proposals for windfarms on the west coast, in the context of the Heritage Council's forthcoming document on landscape policy. Unfortunately the question has become extremely urgent and cannot wait upon longterm consideration.... I am reluctant to involve myself in this matter, but, having mapped the Aran Islands in great detail and written so much about them, I feel a degree of personal responsibility for the preservation of their particular qualities. So I am writing to the Comharchumainn of each of the three islands asking them not to go down this road of wind-power, despite its superficially 'green' credentials. There are places in which windfarms could be sited without much visual pollution, but the Aran Islands are not among them. In particular the Atlantic coastline, from the lighthouse in Inis Oírr to the one on An tOileán Iarthach at the western end of the island chain, is by any standards quite exceptional, and is virtually uninterrupted and unspoiled. Because this is a landscape of bare stone and the strata run horizontally, its skylines are stark and simple and all the subsidiary landforms harmonize with them in a spacious unity. The experience of walking the clifftops, or of approaching the seaboard down one of the islands' narrow walled boreens, is profound. One is confronted by the drama of the natural world – the violence of storms, the endurance of rock, and the strange and subtle ways in which birds and plants find living-space between these mighty opposites.

But despite its grandeur this is a very vulnerable landscape. Its perspec-

tives are long and wide open. Anything sticking up above the field walls is visible from far away. Nothing could be more destructive to it than the endless gesticulations of windmills. If such an interruption is sanctioned anywhere along the length of that coast the continuity will be broken, and other threatened intrusions will be harder to resist....

I sent similar letters to other papers and to the three island co-operatives; and later, when it was clear that no change of heart had been effected in the Inis Meáin Co-operative by my arguments, the letter became the basis of my objection to the granting of planning permission. But the Galway County Council planners were similarly unmoved, and granted permission, so I had hastily to contact the various environmentalist organizations and persuade them to appeal the decision. The only reply from the islands at that stage was an abusive letter in the local paper from my old bugbear the Connemara politician, who was now the prime mover in the windfarm project. I copy out a few sentences only, the whole being too long and garbled to bear reproduction.

As Manager of Inis Meáin Community Co-op, and as a committed promoter of natural resource development aimed at copper fastening a viable and sustainable island community on Inis Meáin, I am happy to be branded as a potential desecrator by the Archangel environmentalist and self-styled protector of the folding landscapes of Connemara and the Aran Islands.... I have come to the conclusion that David Bellamy-like Robinson has a serious problem with the cultural and heritage attitudes as expressed by Connemara people and Aran Islands people.... If he is still hell-bent on depopulating Inis Meáin beyond viability, and if he still wants to frustrate the twenty six years of Comharchumann Inis Meáin Teo to keep the island community alive and vibrant, it would be advisable that he seek a mandate from the islanders for whom he feels such a degree of personal responsibility.

Such rant is easy to reply to, indeed to take advantage of, in the rough-and-tumble genre of Letters to the Editor, but it does find its audience among the ill-informed. Soon after this appeared I happened to visit a remote cottage in Connemara in search of the names of the mountain passes above it, and found that the old farmer who was proud to help me record his fast-fading oral lore was also convinced that I wanted to drive him and his like out of Connemara! But I also heard from several Inis Meáin islanders opposed to the windfarm scheme who were as sad and angry as I am about the degeneration in the look of the island over recent years, and a founder member of the Co-op, Tarlach de Blácam, resigned in protest against its manager's unauthorized response to my observations and joined the campaign against the proposal. But, knowing the spite that can fester in small isolated communities, I refrained from causing any further divisions in Inis Meáin.

As it happened I visited the island soon afterwards for the opening of the newly restored 'Synge's Cottage', in which, a hundred years ago, Synge, Pearse and other seekers for the true Ireland used to lodge. I reported on my impressions in another letter to the *Connacht Tribune*:

... *The next day some of us strolled down to the deserted south coast of the island. The maze of little fields with its superb backdrop of the Atlantic horizon and the Cliffs of Moher had never looked lovelier. To our delight we saw a sea eagle (the first to be sighted in the Aran Islands?) sailing low over the stone walls, accentuating the wild magnificence of the scene. But then we were heartbroken to find that half a mile or so of the boreen had recently been sprayed with weedkiller and was a strip of brown desert among all this beauty. This particular boreen is to be the access road for the projected windfarm – and I noted that from immediately beyond the windfarm site the rest of the boreen is full of wildflowers: ox-eye daisies, tall spires of yellow agrimony, bloody cranesbill and dozens of other species, among which hundreds of burnet moths were just emerging from their chrysalises. Surely something deeply wrong is going on here, morally wrong in terms of our relationship to a very wonderful natural and cultural landscape. And surely those founders of modern Ireland whose memory we were celebrating at Synge's Cottage would have been appalled by it! … I hope that the Co-op will turn back from this wrong turning in the history of the island. And I am encouraged in this hope by the Co-op's contribution to the work on Synge's Cottage, which has shown its ability to care for the island in the right way.*

Neither my emollient remarks about the Co-op nor my appeal to the ghosts of the national ancestors caused a change of heart in the proponents of the scheme, but the neighbouring island of Inis Oírr responded to my open letters by inviting me to address a seminar on forward planning. I accepted with deep misgivings, fearing the occasion might become acrimonious, for the speakers were to include my Connemara politician and the head of the Galway Alternative Energy Centre, a forceful young man who sniffs breezes appreciatively, saying 'Ah! Kilowatt-hours!' But the debate was well chaired, and it gave me an opportunity to amplify my direct appeal to the islanders:

WHAT'S SO SPECIAL ABOUT ARAN?

In making decisions about our own little patches of the Earth's surface and how we are to live on it, we have to bear in mind a wider background. The Earth's population has doubled in the lifetime of most of us here today. Every one of us wants more in the way of material goods and such immaterial ones as mobility and choice. Humanity is exerting an immense, unparalleled, pressure on the resources of the earth, including Lebensraum, *living-space. But these resources are limited; what we take, other forms of life lose. Hundreds and thousands of plant and animal species are going out of existence because there is no space, no peace, no nature for them to flourish in; we are presiding over and responsible for one of the most rapid mass extinctions in the whole geological history of the planet.*

Coming a little closer to home, in Ireland the landscape is changing more rapidly than ever before. Roads, housing estates, forestry, turf extraction, quarrying, are eating up the natural biological surface of the land day by day. And what is left is losing its naturalness. The hilltops have masts on them, the wide spaces of the bogs are rimmed by lines of pylons, the bays are dotted with fish cages. All these things are there to fulfil our demands; we are all implicated. But we should be aware of the cost. In a word, the world is getting smaller and smaller. Each place is becoming more and more like every other place. History is being bulldozed out of the way. Even the most familiar birds – thrushes, skylarks – and the common butterflies, are being poisoned out of existence. Our youngsters probably think that wildlife is a TV show. Technology flourishes and exerts its fascination; the rest of life is becoming less and less interesting and beautiful.

I feel we are reaching the crisis of this stage of humanity's life cycle, and that perhaps in another generation a more intelligent technology and more caring attitudes to the rest of creation will assert themselves. So what we have to do at this juncture is to hold on to what we still have, and fight to protect it from destruction. The key to rural development is to preserve the best aspects of the rural environment, the features that make it attractive and lovely to live in as compared to the urban environment. If the countryside becomes just a poor imitation of suburbia, people will leave it for the real thing. But I also believe it is a duty, a moral obligation, for people who have the privilege of living in, say, a beautiful old city or a lovely countryside, to conserve and enhance it for the good of the whole of humanity.

Focusing in on the Aran Islands, what we have here is one of the strangest and most interesting places in the world. Humanity and nature working on each other for centuries have brought forth a landscape which is not paralleled anywhere else in the world. Its combination of grandeur of scale in the natural and fineness of detail in the human contribution, is literally unique. So, if Aran is indeed special, it demands special consideration and sensitivity in planning. For instance, the scale and the details of the network of boreens are important. I hesitate to revisit a lot of little corners of the islands that I know so well, in case they are gone, like the lovely Róidín Ard leading out towards Synge's Chair in Inis Meáin, a loss which I know many islanders deeply regret. Recently I've been campaigning against the proposal to site three wind turbines on the south shore of Inis Meáin. The argument for wind power is of course that it is non-polluting, doesn't contribute to global warming etc. I'm as concerned as anyone about the long-term threats to our environment from fossil fuels. But there is no use saying wind turbines are non-polluting; they are grossly visually polluting, at least in some landscapes. The three relevant features of wind turbines are:

1) the obvious one, that they are very tall and can be seen for miles, especially in an open landscape that is composed of long level horizons like this.

2) that they are always in motion, so they draw the eye and you can't get away from them.

3) that they are all more or less the same – they are industrial products, and so they tend to reduce all the different landscapes they occur in to the same sort of homogenized uniformity.

Now in the West we have a series of very delicate, very special and very fragile landscapes, which we are likely to lose rather quickly if the present rush to install windfarms persists. Some hard decisions are needed about where they should be put and where not. I'm glad to say that since the Inis Meáin project came up, a national debate on that question has begun. But it doesn't need a debate to see that Aran is the last place they should be permitted. That would be a rank exploitation of Aran's environment.

I ended by quoting the 'Afterwords' of a little book I'd published to accompany my map of the islands:

Step into one of Aran's fourteen thousand little fields, and you are back in the nineteenth century. Walk the Atlantic cliffs, and the ramparts of Dún Aonghasa startle by their modernity. Stroll down the boreens, and you go arm in arm with the Atlantic, for their pattern is that of the fissures caused by the forces that separated Europe from America sixty or seventy million years ago. The Aran Islanders are inescapably face-to-face with the elemental and the timelessly recurrent, from the spray of winter storms to the foam of daisies in springtime pastures.

Thus, Aran is one of civilization's loftiest windows onto its own origins in the past and the natural world. In addition to the economic and social penalties of being marginal to material Europe, the Aran community bears the responsibility of keeping that window crystal clear for ever. Since throughout Europe we have let such windows become blurred and dingy, Aran has the right to call on the wider community, national and international, for whatever support it needs in its priestlike task. Nowadays, with so much of its surface in wreckage and filth, it is the Earth that faces us with moral demands. The spiritual merges once again with the natural, from which, disastrously, it has been separated for some centuries.

However, nobody lives on this glorious, elemental, level all the time;

in Aran one is also simply exposed to the elements, that is, rained-on, fogbound, windblown, cut off. Life is tough, opportunities limited. Improvement of the economic basis is the natural and rightful expectation of the people. At the same time, like it or not, a special trust is invested in them. If islands lose their singularity, the world becomes smaller. If Aran, in offering us more and more of the comforts and facilities of the outskirts of Galway, reduces the possibility of escaping from the banalities of suburban life, we are all impoverished, in our relationship to the past, to nature, to the influence of solitude and space. There may be specific developments that in other places would be welcome and proper, and that Aran should forgo. To live on Aran is a rare and demanding privilege; it is to be the inheritor of something both awkward and valuable, like a Stradivarius, or intangible, like a talent that only rewards long commitment.

In concluding this work, the last and best I can do for Aran, I thank the islanders for seconding my efforts over the years, and commend these precious islands to their good sense.

In the old days the islanders had to put up with priests coming out to conduct missions featuring bloodcurdling sermons against making poitín and reading the books of Liam O'Flaherty. I think they forgave the mildly preacherly tone of this appeal addressed not to their faithful souls but to their 'good sense'; at any rate there was applause and a cry of 'Hear, hear!'

Since that occasion, the Planning Board has rejected the appeal against the granting of planning permission, dismissing all our patient documentation of the splendours of the island landscape with a phrase to the effect that the development would not interfere with the visual attractions of the place. Their Inspector's Report included this fatuity on the aesthetics of the question:

> On a calm sunny day this area has a wonderful environmental quality with beautiful colours but the reality is that it experiences very frequent rainfall, showers, grey skies and heavy seas. In that context I consider that a small windfarm development might well be considered as being complementary to the character of this landscape in that it would be perceived as utilizing the obviously available wind resource.

So, since the Inis Meáin turbines are regarded as a test case, we can now expect an infestation of these demented clockwork giants throughout the windy West.

★

But what antiques, revenants, freakshows they will be, the little patches such as Aran and Roundstone Bog, if we succeed in saving them while the avalanche of metal and concrete covers all the rest! Everybody will come to admire them, which will wear them to ribbons, or they will be off-limits to all but their custodians. There will certainly be no room for Atlantic hermits like myself; we would be elbow to elbow from the North Cape of Norway to Gibraltar.

Weighing the boxes of documentation generated by these two skirmishes – parochial but exemplary – against the daily headlines on the worldwide advance of destruction, I am not so confident as my words in Inis Oírr suggest, about the survivability of the coming crisis and the caring regime that is to follow. Seen from space our globe shows scars, circular geological features resulting from asteroid impacts; they are called 'astroblemes'. Most of these are millions of years old; all the more recent blemishes of Earth are due to human trampling. The imagery of the step that has sustained me through so much writing on the Echosphere is becoming uncomfortable; it transmits pain. What might be called anthropoblemes (horrible word for horrible things) can be felt through the soles of one's feet. But, outside of Gaian fantasies, the Earth itself does not suffer; we are its nerve-cells, its pain is ours. The other creatures of the Earth bear it individually to their varying capacities for suffering, and we humans alone can feel it in its generality, as is only fitting. For our footprint is, in ecological terms, 'loss of biodiversity', wearing-thin of the weave of life as one species after another declines into rarity, singularity, and final extinction (which means, for the sentient and sociable among them, some last impoverished life and solitary death). We accomplish this unprecedented massacre of the innocents by interrupting nature's cycles, denying it space for its patterns, time for its adjustments. And now, if nature has to be subsumed into technics to ensure our own survival, if conservation of the wild is to become mere landscape gardening, then my echopoetry is only nostalgia and I have invested my heart in dandelion fluff.

These are dreadful considerations. They embitter the waters of the West for me; they are in themselves a pollution. I am tempted to retreat from them into the domestic, or take flight into Pascalian infinities.

A HOUSE ON A SMALL CLIFF

The four creatures, as disparate as the corners of a square, who live in this house spend most winter evenings symmetrically disposed about the small wood-burning stove that stands for our hearth. M and I occupy wing-chairs (I was intolerant of their bourgeois solidity when my parents bought them in the fifties, but I appreciate their comfort now), hers facing a glass door into the conservatory that also functions as a front porch, and mine the window, its green-velvet curtains drawn against the north wind tonight, that looks out onto the quayside. The cat and the dog (a fluffy short-legged terrier about the size of the cat) curl up in baskets to right and left of the stove, showing no preferences between them; sometimes there is a little wrangling for the space between the legs of the stove, where the cat in particular relishes very high temperatures but the dog soon begins to pant and has to be ordered out to cool off.

This is our winter-room and library. It is about twelve feet square and disproportionately high, having a coved ceiling with a skylight in the north-east corner. Above the stove is a mantelpiece with a cloisonné vase, midnight blue and peach blossom, which I think must have come from my grandmother's antique shop, and a fake carriage clock that came free with a purchase from a mail-order catalogue. Between these hangs an oval rosewood mirror which from my chair shows a reflection of the skylight, empty black by night, or star-dotted or streaked with silvery rivulets of rain; as I begin to write this, on midwinter eve, the full moon appears in the mirror, stealing my warmth, instilling a Mallarméean chill. I have never seen the moon in this way before; it must be exceptionally high in the north-eastern sky. The papers say it is nearer the earth tonight than it has been for a century.

The library holds some few thousand books, none of much individual market value but collectively irreplaceable, the product of browsing in bookstalls and jumble-sales. Those shelved on either side of the fireplace have been placed there for appearance; they have a bit of gilt or a pattern on the back, or pleasing titles like *She Cometh Up As a Flower* and *She Might Have Been a Duchess*, both from M's collection of nineteenth-century women's novels. In a recess to the left are 'recent acquisitions', mostly bought from catalogues of remaindered books and astonishingly heterogeneous. Among them at the moment are *The Distribution of Prime Numbers*, which will join a shelf of mathematics texts and popular science books once I have resigned myself to the fact that it is too advanced for me; a paperback of Cormac McCarthy's blood-boltered novel about the wolf, abandoned at the point where M could not bear to read on; and all the volumes except the last of Carmichael's *Carmina Gadelica*, a trophy of my recent visit to the Hebrides. Over the window is a five-foot-long shelf with a slight sag in the middle; most of it is taken up by books of an environmentalist persuasion, and the rest by a collection of various editions of my own writings; I tend to glance up at this and worry that the row is not longer. The next wall, opposite the fireplace, is largely literature, and roughly in alphabetical order. A browser would soon notice that no women writers are represented, because they have all been commandeered by M for her feminist collection shelved on the fourth wall of the room; we sometimes discuss reintegration, but that would be a major ideological shift and a day's dusty work.

Leaving the warmth of the library to go to bed, we pass through a corner of the livingroom next to it, which is enormous, impossible to heat for winter use, with wide windows along the north side and another in the eastern gable end, all giving onto the waters and farther shores of Roundstone Bay. We glance down its chilly perspective as we hurry through, or if the night is fine go to the gable window to admire the patterns of moon-ridden wavelets and listen to an oyster-catcher's lonesome whistle flitting to and fro in the blackness. By day this room is entranced by its views; entertaining guests here on summer evenings we sometimes find that a companionable silence falls, all of us lapsing into reverie over the mountains' slow rebuilding of themselves out of dusk after having spent their substance in sparkles all day long. There are trays of seedlings on the wide windowledges, and M's several fancy sorts of fuchsia in pots on the floor. The furniture is heterogeneous and undistinguished, the ornaments are all accidental acquisitions given to us by visiting children or bought to fill an empty minute in a Clifden junkshop, but the general effect is spacious and pleasing, our *forté* as home-makers, we sometimes think, being the nice arrangement of the nasty. The room has three skylights and the same high board-lined ceiling as the library, which was evidently divided off from it by a thin partition wall at some stage.

A hundred years ago the whole chamber was one of the Lace

Schools set up by the Congested Districts Board here and there throughout its poverty-stricken fiefdom under the charitable patronage of the Viceroy's wife, Lady Aberdeen. A young lady from Fermanagh, Margaret Cosgrove, came to teach the craft here, and married Richard O'Dowd, clerk to the landlord's agent, who had his office next door on the quayside; their descendants still own O'Dowd's, the summer visitors' favourite bar and restaurant, overlooking the harbour, and when we took over this building and began to rescue it from years of dereliction, one of them gave us a photograph of Margaret and her two sisters, also lace-teachers, one employed in Ros Muc and other villages of Connemara and the other in Cliffony, County Sligo, all three wearing wondrous evening gowns of their own creation.

That photograph hangs by the gable window of the big room, together with others relating to an earlier stage in its history when, according to the oldest resident of Roundstone, it was the ballroom of someone called 'Sainty' Robinson, of whom she knew no more than his intriguing name. I was anxious to find out more of him, foreseeing that I will be conflated with him in folk-memory if there still is such a thing in another century's time. It seemed likely that he was a connection of George Robinson and his son, who were successively land agents for most of Connemara from the 1850s to the 1930s and lived in Letterdyfe House just north of Roundstone. But I could establish nothing about him, until one evening there was a knock on our door, and an elderly gentleman of Edwardian mien greeted me with 'Mr Robinson? – *I'm* Robinson!' This Dr Philip Robinson of Dublin, who turned out to be descended from George Robinson, had heard tell that his forebear had been a harsh, evicting agent, and was calling on me as a local historian to find out if this was so. I took him down to the studio, opened my files and showed him the evidence that it was indeed so. Nevertheless we became fast friends, to the point that we found ourselves almost adopted into the posterity of the Letterdyfe Robinsons, and inheritors, after Dr Philip's death, of several memorabilia of the family. So it comes about that I can identify 'Sainty' in a copy of the family tree as a St-John Robinson, one of George's younger sons, and that a pair of framed Victorian silhouettes of George and his wife Rebecca hang in Sainty's former ballroom. And once a year, on the day of Roundstone Regatta, we remind the room of its past, hold open house and drink to the dancers of old. While the traditional work-boats, the Galway hookers, gather below our windows to race in the bay, an extraordinary mix of guests drop in for a lunch of courgette eggah and apple crumble, watch the events from our windows, go off to crew a boat or join the crowd of spectators on the quayside, and return for tea. Sometimes a visiting poet recites, musicians bring out their fiddles and flutes, ladies from the village dance a Connemara set; sometimes when we sit down with a few lingering guests, the evening is mellow with wine and the last of the red-brown sails are ghosting home to the harbour through a pearly mist, there are moments in this room when time itself is perfectly content.

The rest of this level of our house is an extension to the back, probably added when the building became a knitting factory under the regime of a State development body, Gaeltarra Éireann, in the 1950s. First comes a space we have turned into a kitchen, originally an office separated from the big room by a glazed screen through which the supervisor used to keep an eye on her workforce, as several elderly ladies of the village well remember. From there a corridor leads back, with cookery and gardening books shelved on the left, and on the right, two windows onto a small rockery under a misshapen cypress that leans close to the house, called Crann na gCat, the cats' tree, because cats, our cat and her visitors, love to lie along its broad, comfortable branches. There are circular jumble-sale mirrors looking each way along this corridor; in fact the house has so many mirrors, glazed doors and windows that a diagram of how scraps of sky and garden are multiplied within it would look like that of an optical instrument. And since the sea surrounds us on the north and east, whatever light falls into the house from those quarters is accompanied – shadowed – by a thin restless inverse of itself flung upwards onto ceilings.

At the end the corridor turns left into the bedroom, from which a portion has been glassed off as M's room: her Italian books, the ironing-board, her desk, and in a drawer the backup copies of my writings, to be snatched to safety in the garden in case of fire. Our bed is very wide, on a low platform homemade out of planks and two-by-one timber; there is room for entwining and room for being untouched, surface area for books and breakfast tray, and for Squig the dog who sleeps nested against the curve of M's back; Nimma the cat sleeps in the library but sometimes joins us in the morning and curls up under my caressing hand while I read the paper. Lying in bed we are facing two windows and a glass-panelled door onto the garden; we watch the seasonal transformations of an ancient hawthorn tree against the minute-by-minute transformations of the sky. Morning sunlight beams in, glowing in the leaves and blossoms of geraniums on the window ledges as in stained glass. One or two friends who know our late-morning ways sometimes follow the path round the house to the garden door, and if they find it as is usual wide open, come in to sit in chairs opposite us, as at a *Petit Lever*. All is *luxe, calme et volupté*, with a good deal of the often forgotten ingredient, *ordre*. Finally there is the bathroom, narrow, with two little square windows at the far end like picture frames holding trial-pieces of the hour and its weather.

We are house-proud, and garden-proud. First-time visitors would not know we had a garden other than the shady rockery under the cypress by the front door; in fact the topography would not seem to provide room for more. So if we want to amaze them we bring them through the house to the garden door, where it is as if space had suddenly sprouted a new dimension. A rather undulating and irregular lawn leads away down a long perspective between, on the left, a high, ragged, thunder-dark fuchsia hedge, and on the right a sequence of incidentals – paths curving out of sight between raised flowerbeds, a garden hut overwhelmed by honeysuckle, a little sunset mountain-range of hydrangeas, a grove of a dozen birchtrees – that demand to be explored. We respond to that demand every day except when the rain is heavy; we carry our mugs of coffee around in a ritual that includes the animals, Squig bounding ahead and looking back with a ball in her mouth, Nimma sauntering after as if it were only by chance she had decided to look round the garden at the same time as us. We commend every blossom in its burgeoning and fall; we allow ourselves to be amazed again and again, like a child with a favourite story-book, by the sequence of the seasons.

The paths are odd, being made of rectangular concrete blocks, which soon lose their harsh blue-grey tone and sharp edges as moss takes them in hand, and are easily dug up and reset when I decide to realign a path, as I frequently do. These narrow ways fork and loop and duck under trees around a dozen little subsections of the garden in a romantic, even sentimental, way, and then unexpectedly – even to us, who made all this – straighten themselves up into the perimeter of a slightly sunken, square, parterre, the centre of which is marked very formally by the slim vertical of a cordyline palm. This forum, as we call it, is surrounded by aspens and birches and larches, which screen it from the new holiday apartments overlooking us from inland but are slender enough to leave it sunny, and one can sit in still air here even when the rest of Connemara is hysterical with gales. Its area is divided up by a symmetrical pattern of 144 concrete blocks into 145 square plots of earth, 81 of them defined by the long edges of four blocks and 64 by short edges, the larger plots being regularly interspersed with the smaller ones. In the 32 plots nearest the edge, all the way round, we grow extravagant amounts of parsley from which once a year we make jamjarfuls of a sweet jelly called parsley honey, and in the others are chives, mint, blue corydalis, pink oxalis and so on, in an irrational and planless mixture. This numerological garden was a work I undertook at a time when I was spending long nerve-stretching hours every day dotting details onto my Connemara map with a magnifying glass; in the evenings I would restore a sense of scale to my muscles and bones by digging out barrowloads of earth and levering the heavy blocks into position with the back of a spade. It has settled itself comfortably into the ground, weather has gentled it and fernspores have discovered its crevices, so that it already looks as if it has been there for a hundred years. Walking across it, feeling the regularity it imposes on the step, reminds me of Aran's fissured limestone flags, and of the 'wavy concrete floor', the unrealized project of my London days.

If every garden has a secret, that of our garden is the sea.

Behind the fuchsia hedge the ground falls almost sheerly for eighteen feet or so to the seashore. Gaps in the hedge give us irregular windows onto the waters of the bay, and when one of Roundstone's half-deckers goes by one hears waves on the rocks below discussing the event for some minutes afterwards. There is a little patio outside the garden door, and from a corner of this one can lean over a wooden rail and look along the cliff face, a tangle of brambles and nettles, with ledges settled by sea-pink from nature below and montbretia from culture above.

The cliff meets the gable end of the house at an angle and seems to disappear; it is difficult to make out how it is folded into the structure of the building. This becomes clearer when one goes round to the other side, past the conservatory or front porch, where a broad flight of steps descends to a courtyard between our inland gable and the apartments next door. From here one can see that the nucleus of the building has two stories and is built against the cliff; the upper storey with its old slate roof looks like a long cottage, and consists of our library and the big sea-room, with the extension running back from it at clifftop level. The lower storey also has an extension, to the front, at sea-level. There is no interior communication between upstairs and downstairs. Above is our home, which we call Nimmo House after the Scots engineer who founded Roundstone in the 1820s, built the pier just outside the courtyard gate and may have had a store on this site; below is the premises of Folding Landscapes, publishers of maps, archivists of local lore, lookers-out at the sea. When we acquired the building in 1989 it had long been in use as a rubbish dump and store for a dreadful knitting factory next door, which had gone into bankruptcy and is now replaced by the holiday apartments. The front extension in particular was a concrete shell, a dismal clutter of windowless cells, broken-down garage doors, rusty boilers. Penetrating its filthy corridors we found at the back a huge room the low ceiling of which had partly collapsed onto the heaps of plastic bags full of reject woollen socks that almost filled it. The rear wall of this dank cavern masks the cliff face. Nowadays Folding Landscapes is full of light that floods through many windows, interior openings and glass screens, but I am still aware of the cliff it is founded on, that has not been seen since Nimmo's time, or at least since the Robinsons of Letterdyfe had turf-stores and sheds for carts and pony-traps here, and I imagine it waiting, unresignedly, until we have all gone away.

THE FINENESS OF THINGS

Once, looking out into the poplartree that tapped with hundreds of triangular leaves at a window of our first-floor flat in London, I saw a small furry caterpillar. I have always been fond of such creatures, so I opened the window and collected it into a jamjar. It had a creamy stripe down the back from which four tufts of brownish hairs stood up like a liner's funnels, and longer sheaves of hairs stuck out in front of it and to the rear. I still possess my 1946 reprint of Richard South's *Moths of the British Isles*, probably the most intensively read book of my childhood, and from it I was able to identify this curiosity as the larva of a Vapourer Moth – 'quite a Cockney insect, and found in almost every part of the Metropolis where there are a few trees'. A few days later it retired among the leaves I had given it to feed on, spun up its cocoon, and pupated. I left the jamjar open on a windowledge, and a month or so afterwards noticed that the moth had emerged and crawled out of the jar, and was clinging to the inside of the windowpane. It – she – was a poor-looking, greyish spider-like object; the female of this species is wingless. She was motionless, apparently inert. I raised the sash window a few inches to see if fresh air might invigorate her.

By a marvellous chance later in the day I was passing through the room and happened to glance out just as a small moth came flying towards the window from across the lawn. Its course was slightly irregular and side-slipping, but as purposeful as a saw biting through wood. It shot in through the gap under the sash, went across the room and down to the floor, where it fumbled and tumbled, gradually back-tracking to the window and eventually finding its goal after many dartings and near-misses. It – he – was a bright-winged little creature, red-ochre with a whitish spot on the trailing edge of each forewing. They clung together immediately, and she began to lay her eggs as they mated, egg after egg after egg, her body slackening and thinning, until after a few hours and about two hundred eggs, she was empty, spent, dead.

One of the hundred threads of implication one could tease out from this passionately observed event – like all such, a knot of parables – is that the transparent space above our lawn that day was seething with messages. The male moth had been able to lock onto the plume of eroticism emanating from the female, which if it had been visible would have looked like a wavering magic carpet unrolled through the air from the narrow slit under the window sash. Simultaneously, countless other insects, indifferent to the Vapourer's aphrodisiac effluvium, had followed the scent of their own destinies across the garden. But these pheromones – externalized hormones that co-ordinate, and sometimes destabilize, social and sexual behaviour – are not peculiar to insects; from the single-celled protozoan partaking in a slime-slow conglomeration with indefinite numbers of its like, to the rational human being flustered by a *je-ne-sais-quoi* wafted into the margins of consciousness by another's passing-by, we all are subject to their persuasions. The substance secreted by the female Vapourer's sex-glands is known to the specialist as (z)-6-Heneicosene-11-one (there is a web site on which one can find such recondite information). Its molecules are built of twenty-one atoms of carbon, thirty-eight of hydrogen and one of oxygen, combined in a specific shape; they go twirling through the jostling throng of lesser molecules constituting air until, perhaps a mile away, some of them happen to fall into the right position to fit the equally specific shape of receptor molecules in cells of the male Vapourer moth's antennae. Pheromones are clouds of keys, drifting at random; but in such billions they will find their locks.

The Cockneys' mating took place in high summer: the Earth was rounding that part of its orbit where its northern regions are favourably inclined towards the sun by day, splendid energies were being lavished on the Metropolis, and sequences of influences we hardly know about had primed the moths to multiply while food for the next generation was green and juicy. What are the proportions between these realms, of the solar system and the moths' sexual chemistry? When I was a child my fond parents wrote a rhyme in which they boasted: 'Tim will discover stars / forty times as big as Mars!', and although I may have disappointed them in that respect, I have learned something of the relative scales of things. The diameters of the smaller planets such as Mars and Earth stand to my height in roughly the same ratio as I do to a single cell of my body, while stars, like molecules, figure in ranges much remoter from the human scale. It is only in a very narrow range that we have a natural sense of size. The degree of smallness that most impresses us is, by a perspective effect, the closest to us; not the microbial or atomic but that of objects a tiny but appreciable fraction of our own size, down as far as dust-motes, the vanishing points of the domestic. In folktales a sprinkling of 'fernseed' renders one invisible, and indeed the size of fernspores marks one of the two exits from the world of naturally visible objects. The further reaches of smallness, like the figures astronomy offers for galactic distances, fade into the abstract, the inconceivable, the incomprehensible. Contemplation of these two vistas led Pascal to his magnificent meditation on the abysses between which the human being is suspended:

Let man contemplate the whole realm of nature in its full and exalted majesty; let him lift his glance to this dazzling light, placed like a lamp to illumine the universe to all eternity; let the earth appear to him but as a point in the vast circle described by this luminary, and let him pause to wonder at the fact that this vast circle is itself but a tiny point compared to that described by the stars revolving in the firmament. But if man's view be arrested there, let his imagination pass beyond.... This whole visible world is but a speck on the broad bosom of nature.... It is a sphere, whose centre is everywhere, and its circumference nowhere....

But to show him another marvel, no less astonishing, let him consider a mite, and note the tiny body composed of parts incomparably more minute; the limbs with joints, the veins in the limbs, blood in the veins, humours in the blood, drops in the humours, and vapours in the drops. Let him again divide these parts, and he may think he has arrived at the most extreme diminutive in nature. Then I will open before him a new abyss. I will depict for him not only the visible universe, but all the immensity of nature imaginable, in the enclosing envelope of this minute atom. Let him see therein an infinity of universes, each with its firmament, planets, and earth in the same proportions as in the visible world.... Our human body, just now perceived to be but an imperceptible atom in an insignificant planet of the universe, now becomes a world, with regard to the nothingness into which we cannot penetrate. Whoever sees himself in this way will be terrified of himself, and, considering how he is upheld in the material substance nature has given him between the two abysses of the infinite and the nothing, he will tremble at the sight of such marvels.

Awe-inspiring as this is, and profound in its anticipation of so much that has been established or hypothesized since his day, I feel that it runs off to infinity too readily, too tendentiously; Pascal is frightening us into the arms of God. Believing that for good or ill our life is totally of this universe, I will look down these perspectives again.

Powers of ten are a useful way of keeping one's head in plumbing these dizzy gulfs. Let multiplication by ten and division by ten be taken as steps up and down, respectively, in the scale of lengths; then one step up from me is the height of a big house, two steps, representing a factor of a hundred, is a hill, three a mountain, four the distance across a town, five a great city, six a country, seven the diameter of the Earth. Downwards, one step brings me to the rat, two to the moth, three to its egg, four to a single iridescent scale of its wing, five to the single-celled forms of life. Already I need instruments to extend my senses. In exploring my landscapes in the West I have often called on scientists to show me how much I'm missing, and what they let me glimpse through their microscopes is astounding in its variety and complexity. A drop of pondwater from the Burren is a toy-chest of darting, wriggling, lumbering, colliding, shunting, contraptions so ingenious in their modes of locomotion one is struck by the absence of the wheel; some of the busiest of these untiring searchers are single-celled algae, photosynthesists, therefore members of the plant kingdom. In Connemara, Dog's Bay has a white beach mainly composed of the shells of Foraminifera, single-celled animals that draw calcium carbonate out of seawater and use it to make themselves external skeletons. Each sort – and about 200 species have been recorded here to date – builds to its own design, and these tend to the fantastic, the obsessive and the absurd, at least to our eyes accustomed to reading human purposes into artefacts: I see among them cakes from confectionery competitions, fretted globes of Chinese ivory-work, spiky hot-water bottles. Praeger, in whose books I first read about this beach and saw Foraminifera shells illustrated, wondered how each of these minute blobs of jelly knows what sort of shell it is supposed to produce. Nowadays at least parts of the answer are known in outline, in terms of instructions encoded in DNA, interference patterns of chemicals flowing across cell surfaces, and so on.

I will also mention the fossil pollen grains preserved at various levels in bogs and lake sediments, from which palaeoecologists can reconstruct the plantlife of landscapes long gone under the ground. Pollen, that aerial silk, epitome of what is dispersed as irrecoverably as breath, is one of nature's toughest products; long after root and bark have rotted, pollen remains and keeps every detail of its species characteristics. Hazel pollen is a plump triangular cushion with a pore like a porthole at each corner; pine has two reticulated airbags to help it drift far and wide, that give it the appearance of a fly's head; elm is almost spherical, with five pores evenly spaced around a circumference, and a brain-like surface pattern. So we know that in about 3800 BC when Neolithic settlers first cleared the forest around Lough Sheeauns in north-west Connemara, the ribwort plantain sprang up, a wildflower reinventing itself as a weed of cultivation. But it is not the specifics of such knowledge that astound me, it is its quality of specificity, the fineness of detail with which the world records itself and in which its records can be read, through the optics and insights of the various sciences.

Looking outwards, perhaps the order of planetary movements, insofar as we see them inscribed upon the sphere of night, answers to that of fernseed in the inward perspective. And that is why astrology arises here, at the apparent limits of naturally comprehensible space, making our inner selves visible as fernseed makes our outer selves invisible. The theory of the direct influence on our characters and careers of the planets' 'aspects' at the moment of our births, the whole creaking medieval apparatus of oppositions, conjunctions, sextiles, squares and trines, is inconsistent with both the findings of science and its selfcritical procedures; as a phenomenon of contemporary culture it lies on dodgy ground between counselling and bingo. However, when I say this to an astrologer friend she replies, weakly but indefeasibly, 'But it works!' If so, that is because astrological lore – the never-quite-repetitious starry cycles and all that has been piled up in writing on them since Sumeria – is a rich enough archive of patterns to suit any interpretation; we project onto it hopes and fears that we cannot face directly, and then can recognize them, like Leonardo's faces of all humanity read into the stains on a wall.

Far beyond this delusive order, and the related one of the constellations, that index to world mythology, is the reality of the solar system. Eight steps up in the scale of powers of ten from the human body bring us only halfway to the moon; the orbits of the inner planets including Earth lie around the eleventh step; and the outer orbits of the giant planets from Saturn to Neptune, the twelfth. But it would be an equal and opposite mistake to that of astrology, to imagine that the planets pursue their tremendous courses indifferent to our fates; indifference is a human failing, possible only where there is potentiality for caring, and we indulge ourselves in imputing it to the inanimate. In fact we could come to feel affection for these close-to-home features of the solar system, learn to recognize them after a long journey through the comparative emptiness beyond, because they are composed of the same materials as we are, originating probably in a star that once partnered the sun and that ripened and burst and spread its heavy elements about, to be swept together and moulded by gravity and electromagnetism into dust-clouds, asteroids, comets and the planets with their rings, moons, atmospheres, seas and living things. This is not the infinitude of silence that frightened Pascal; this is a space as garrulous, teeming with news and fertile in invention, in its slower tempo, as the air above our lawn on a summer's day.

Such arenas of fruitful interaction are only now beginning to be understood in their general laws; a hierarchy of sciences – chaos theory, complexity theory, new mathematical flesh on the vague old concept of 'emergence' – has recently arisen, itself emerging by the very processes it formalizes out of a chaos and complexity of ideas. The essence of these theories is this, that if a collection of entities is sufficiently numerous and richly interactive, and if it is continually fed with energies that disturb it from sluggish equilibria, eventually parts of it will fall by chance into patterns or cycles that have some capacity for persistence; and if such persistences are continually forthcoming, eventually some will arise that have the property of seeding the development of their like, of replicating themselves; and once there are relatively stable dynamic systems all calling on the same resources of material and energy, they will evolve, be co-opted into systems of higher order. All this is a consequence of a law of large numbers; that if enough things happen, then it is certain that something extremely improbable will happen. Life, intelligence and love are not aliens marooned in a hostile world of iron determinism, doomed to be chilled to death by the dreadful second law of thermodynamics if left unredeemed by the transcendental, as they must have seemed to thinkers of the last century. The furthest developments of these processes, so far as we know and as of today, occur on Earth. A rich enough mix of chemicals, interreacting and fed with heat to keep it far from equilibrium, may spontaneously produce a substance that catalyses other reactions, and then develop more elaborate networks of mutually catalysing processes; hence arises life, hence breeding populations and evolution, hence networks of neurones, thoughts and dreams, social systems that can reflect upon themselves, books that are written to find out what they are about. This is the Eden of autopoiesis, of self-creation; some social-systems theorists claim that Spencer-Brown's *Laws of Form* is its Book of Genesis, and at least one can agree that endlessly reiterated discrimination of one form from another is its dynamics *in abstracto*.

The popularizations of these theories – paradoxically, many of them pioneered in an institute of Santa Fé that is historically downwind from Los Alamos – are among the most liberating texts I have read in recent years. But at a much earlier stage of my life, and in connection with orders of existence one or two steps above and below those just considered, I struggled with those two great intellectual constructions that stand like the Pillars of Hercules at the opening into twentieth-century physics: relativity and quantum theory. It must have been in my middle-school years that I heard Fred Hoyle's BBC talks on the new cosmology; I remember vividly his explaining that the universe is expanding like the surface of a balloon being inflated, of which 'the radius, of course, is Time', and I was particularly struck by that 'of course', which made me want to be on such first-name terms with Time. I read and persuaded myself that I followed Einstein's popular book on relativity, and at least I could appreciate and be amazed at the fact that the famous equation $E = mc^2$ falls out from some comparatively simple mathematics with heart-stopping suddenness. (It expresses the equivalence between energy and mass, c being the speed of light, which is an enormous number, so that c^2 is, one could say, enormously enormous, implying that a stupendous amount of energy can be derived from a very little mass, as had been demonstrated a few years earlier when two cities and their inhabitants were deleted by a few grams of uranium and plutonium, and as we can feel every day from the sunshine on our faces, the sun having been pouring out that flux of radiant energy not just towards the tiny distant dot of the Earth but into all the vastness of space surrounding it, day in day out for millennia, without appreciable loss of substance.)

One or two images from Einstein, in particular that of the observer sitting on a rotating disc as a ray of light passes, which I associate with Tenniel's illustration of the Caterpillar smoking his hookah on a mushroom, still lie in a cupboard of my mind and come to light now and again. The curvature of spacetime as the gravitational effect of mass, and the speculation that our universe may be finite and yet have no bounds, became easier on my brain when I studied Riemann's generalized co-ordinate geometry at Cambridge later on, and it does not distress me that our evolutionarily conditioned powers of visualization are inadequate to them. The more recent postulation and subsequent detection of black holes, formed by an old star collapsing into a little sphere of such density that it draws space closed around itself as if to die in utter seclusion, have for me as a spectator been one of the finest intellectual adventures of our age.

The other great monument of early twentieth-century physics, quantum theory, is conceptually much more testing, and those who really understand it claim that those who claim to understand it show by that very claim that they do not. However, I can see that once again a most dangerous little formula hops out of the mathematics of it at a very early stage: the notorious Uncertainty Principle, $\Delta x . \Delta v \geq h$. To predict the course of an atomic particle, or indeed of any body, one would need accurate information as to its present position and momentum; but the Principle states that the uncertainty of position multiplied by the uncertainty of momentum cannot be reduced below a certain amount, called Planck's Constant, so that if one of these quantities is known very precisely the other can be measured only imprecisely, and vice versa. Hence the future is inherently unpredictable and causality is replaced by probability – not through shortcomings in our understandings or experimental means but as a fundamental feature of the nature of things.

Since Planck's Constant is extremely small these ineluctable uncertainties only begin to become apparent at the atomic level, which begins about nine steps down the scale of powers of ten from everyday life. Quantum theory undoes the comfortable little picture we used to have of atoms as like solar systems, with their electrons circling a nucleus. Rutherford in the 1900s used to claim that he solved problems in electron scattering by asking where he himself would go were he an electron, but in truth another reality underlies the world of solid, handleable, entities our imaginations grew up in, and at our present level of evolution mathematics is the only language that can capture it in detail. A long way further down the scale of powers of ten, far past the nucleus at step fourteen, the Uncertainty Principle upsets the simple negative ideas we have of what Pascal would have called the Void, the perfect vacuum of empty space. The more accurately the time of a process is specified the less predictable is the energy involved. For the extremely short interval in which two atomic particles are in collision, a wild fluctuation of energy can manifest itself as mass in accordance with Einstein's little equation, in fact as a pair of 'virtual' particles, an electron and its opposite, a positron, which flash in and out of existence and can influence the interactions of more normal particles. Thus the 'quantum vacuum' is very different from the utter nothingness of the vacuum as conceived by classical physics; it is a perpetual seethe of being, the source of infinite possibility.

Finally, at what is called the Planck Length, which is about a millionth of a billionth of a billionth of a billionth of a centimetre and corresponds to the thirty-fifth downward step in my schema, the Uncertainty Principle may demolish the continuity of space itself. At this scale, say some theorists, huge momentary concentrations of energy whip space into a froth of self-occlusions analogous to the black holes of astronomy, the concept of length loses its coherence, and one cannot approach any nearer to the dimensionless points conceived in pure geometry. What form of reality underlies this 'quantum foam' is the subject of theories and mathematizations – superstring theory, Penrose's 'twistors' – so recent and advanced, and probably so evanescent, that to summarize my slight understanding of them would be mere name-dropping. But I delight in the knowledge that human thought is already probing this incomprehensible space riddled with riddles.

Strangely, images of foam abound at the other end of the scale of powers of ten. At twenty-one steps above the human measure we have the galaxies, of which our Milky Way, containing a hundred billion stars, is one; at step twenty-four, clusters of thousands of galaxies; at twenty-five, a sheet of clusters of galaxies called the Great Wall, three hundred million light years across. This last was until recently the largest known structure, but now seems to be just one of many such sheets surrounding and separating regions of the universe in which galaxies are rare, like the films of liquid in a mass of bubbles.

One more step brings us to the limit of all we can ever observe, at a distance of about fifteen billion light years or a hundred million billion billion miles – not that there is nothing to observe beyond this limit, which is really one of time set by the fact that light has not had long enough to reach us from any further away, since only fifteen billion years have elapsed since the universe was a dot the size of the Planck Length. 'Is lú na fríde, máthair an oilc,' less than a speck is the mother of evil, an old Aran man told me. Everything we see or ever can see is born of that speck, for good or evil. But, according to one of the most audacious speculations of contemporary cosmology, we may call on the existence of indefinite numbers of other universes to explain the properties of this one, including its manifest ability to support intelligent life. For, as Hoyle pointed out a long time ago, physics cannot derive and has to take as given the values of certain constants (I have mentioned two, the speed of light, and Planck's Constant), and if these were only slightly different from what they are we would not be here to comment on the fact. A universe with other values of the universal constants might be too small and short-lived, or too vast and dilute, for stars to form; or its stars might not last long enough for nuclear fusion within them to forge the large nuclei of atoms such as carbon necessary for life; or the whole story might go awry and fade out in some other way.

For some, this fine tuning of the universal constants is proof that we were meant to be, that the Universe or its Creator had written us or something like us into the plans from the beginning. But there is no need to abandon a thoroughgoing naturalism even at this extremity of the thinkable. A universe that gives rise to stars long-lived enough to form carbon and the other necessaries of life is also going to produce stars that go on to collapse into black holes; and black holes being portions of space that have closed in on themselves and are no longer in contact with the universe they form in, could be the buds of new universes. Suppose that these offspring universes inherit the constants of their progenitor, with slight variations rather as living things do; then universes that fail to thrive and do not produce black holes will not be represented in the next generation, and those that bear plentiful buds will preponderate. So, the reason we find ourselves in a universe hospitable to life is that the vast majority of universes are so, for such universes themselves are prolific breeders.

This heartshaking vision of the grounds of our possibility in a perhaps eternal and infinite profusion of universes is strangely like that of the foam of being we glimpse at the other end of the length-scale. We are not desolate creatures helplessly adrift between two deathly abysses. The perspectives I have sketched span the perilous sea of our universe from shore to shore. They are two wings of not-quite-inconceivable breadth and power, that bear us up for a time. Not for long enough, but for a time.

NOTES

BIRDLIFE (AND A PREFACE)

The fiction 'Two Reminiscences of London 1970' is included in *Tales and Imaginings 1965–98*, forthcoming from Lilliput.

THE CURVATURE OF THE EARTH

Most of this essay appeared as 'The Globe' in *The Irish Review*, No. 25, Winter/Spring 1999-2000.

BALLISTICS

Published in *The Dublin Review*, No. 1, Winter 2000-1.

A CAREER IN ART

'Four-colour Theorem' was described in Peter Joseph and Tim Drever, 'Outside the Gallery System: two projects for Kenwood', *Studio International*, London, June 1969.

The article on 'Moonfield' was published in *Adam International Review*, ed. Miron Grindea, London, 1969.

'Field work 3, A Structured Arena' (the essay on the wavelike floor) was published in *PAGE 14 (Bulletin of the Computer Arts Society)*, London, February 1971, and republished in *element*, No. 6, Mermaid Turbulence, Dublin, 1999.

The 'points' were described in an essay, 'Geometer', published in Tim Robinson, *The View from the Horizon*, Coracle Press, London, 1997.

FIREWALKING

Published in *The Recorder*, Vol. 12, No. 2, New York, Fall 1999, and *The Irish Review*, No. 25, Winter/Spring 1999–2000.

Catherine Nash's review is in *The Journal of Historical Geography*, 1997, Vol. 23, No. 3.

THE EXTREME EDGE

The story by Adalbert Stifter was first published as 'Der heilige Abend' in 1845, and as 'Bergkristall' was included in his *Bunte Steine*, 1853. I thank Barbara Scott for translating it for me. The other books mentioned are: Roy Harrod, *Foundations of Inductive Logic*, London 1956, and E.M. Cioran, *La Tentation d'Exister*, Paris, 1956.

CONSTELLATION AND QUESTIONMARK

Quotations from Pascal and Leibnitz are translated from Blaise Pascal, *Oeuvres Complètes*, ed. Jean Mesnard, Desclée de Brower, 1964.

I learned about Dandelin's proof from Tzu-Pei Chen's web site <www.cs.ubc.ca/spider/tzupie/dandelin.html>, and my Fig. 13 is based on one of the elaborate diagrams on this site.

For the expansion of the universe see Idit Zehavi and Avishai Dekel, 'Evidence for a positive cosmological constant from flows of galaxies and distant supernovae', *Nature*, Vol. 401, 252–4 (1999), and related articles in *Scientific American*, January 1999.

There is a 50-page appendix in English on the four-colour map theorem in: George Spencer-Brown, *Laws of Form / Gesetze der Form*, Bohmeier Verlag, 1997. A new English-language edition of *Laws of Form* is in preparation. For the alternative proof by consideration of the 'uncolourables' see George Spencer-Brown, 'Uncolorable Trivalent Graphs', *Cybernetics and Systems*, Vol. 29, No. 4, Philadelphia, 1998.

THE ECHOSPHERE

'Two Wet Days in Roundstone Bog' (slightly enlarged) appeared in *The Irish Review*, No. 24, Autumn 1999.

A HOUSE ON A SMALL CLIFF

Published in *The Recorder*, Vol. 12, No. 4, Fall 2000.

THE FINENESS OF THINGS

Published in *The Recorder*, Vol. 12, No. 4, Fall 2000.

The web site for moth pheromones is at http://www.pherolist.slu.se. The speculation on Darwinian evolution of universes is from Lee Smolin, *The Life of the Cosmos*, Weidenfeld & Nicolson, London, 1997.